ALCOHOLIC BEVERAGE CONTROL

An Official Study

By

THE JOINT COMMITTEE OF THE STATES TO STUDY ALCOHOLIC BEVERAGE LAWS

1950

ALCOHOLIC BEVERAGE CONTROL

An Official Study

By

THE JOINT COMMITTEE OF THE STATES TO STUDY ALCOHOLIC BEVERAGE LAWS

1950

K

J74

A - 863899

MEMBERS OF THE JOINT COMMITTEE

Who planned the study:

> Owen J. Cleary, *Michigan*
> Dick R. Lane, *Iowa*
> Walter F. Morrison, *Colorado*
> John W. Roach, *Wisconsin*

Who conducted the survey and prepared report:

> Arthur G. Burtnett, *Massachusetts*
> Owen J. Cleary, *Michigan*
> John F. O'Connell, *New York*
> Ray E. Tarbox, *New Hampshire*

Serving until May, 1951:

> Owen J. Cleary, *Michigan*
> John W. Hardy, *Virginia*
> Erwin B. Hock, *New Jersey*
> John F. O'Connell, *New York*
> David H. Prichard, *Wisconsin*
> Ray E. Tarbox, *New Hampshire*

MEMBERS OF THE ADVISORY GROUP

GLOSSARY

ABC	Alcoholic beverage control.
Alcoholic beverages	Mean and include spirits, liquor, wine, beer and cider containing alcohol which are capable of being consumed by a human being.
ATU	The Alcohol Tax Unit of the United States Treasury Department.
Beer	Any fermented beverage manufactured from malt, wholly or in part, or from any substitute therefor.
Control	Alcoholic beverage control.
Control States	Those states which have laws regulating, as distinguished from prohibiting, the alcoholic beverage business.
Dry	Any person, group, or branch of government committed to a position in opposition to the manufacture, sale and distribution of alcoholic beverages under sanction of law; also, any geographical area where such sanction does not exist.
Hearing Officer	Member of an ABC agency of government whose function it is to preside over hearings on license applications or on charges against a licensee, usually charged with the duty of ascertaining facts.
Joint Committee	The Joint Committee of the States to Study Alcoholic Beverage Laws.
Liquor	Any distilled or rectified spirits, brandy, whiskey, rum, gin or cordials, including all dilutions and mixtures thereof.
Monopoly State	Any state which engages in the business of buying and selling alcoholic beverages.
NABCA	The National Alcoholic Beverage Control Association, an organization representing the monopoly states as a group.
NCSLA	The National Conference of State Liquor Administrators, an organization representing the open license states as a group.
Open License State	A state where the alcoholic beverage business operates as a private enterprise under state regulation and control through a system of licensing.
PAS	The Public Administration Service, 1313 East 60th Street, Chicago, Illinois, an organization of consultants, researchers and publishers, whose services are available only to branches, units or agencies of government.

V

Rules	Those enactments of ABC agencies of government, under powers delegated to them by grant of their state legislatures, which enactments are mandatory in form and are binding upon licensees and others when properly promulgated.
Temperance	Habitual moderation in the use of alcoholic beverages which inclines the individual to avoid excessive or harmful use thereof and to refrain from every abuse of the right to consume those beverages.
Wine	Beverage consisting of the product of the normal alcoholic fermentation of the juice of fresh, sound, ripe grapes or, occasionally, other fruit.

FOREWORD

The survey covered by this report was conducted, and this report itself was prepared and printed as the first authoritative work of its kind since repeal of the Eighteenth Amendment. At the time of that historic occurrence, three centuries of experimentation in alcoholic beverage control in this country featuring weakness, inaction, half-way measures, primary or exclusive emphasis on the collection of revenue, political connivance, judicial delay, and the abrogation of the right of citizens to drink in moderation, had attained the status of tragic failure.

Following repeal of the Eighteenth Amendment, laws were enacted by most of the states under conditions requiring haste and expedition. For the foregoing, among other reasons, the importance of the study made by the Joint Committee hardly needs mention here. The survey covered by this report was restricted by deliberate choice of the Joint Committee to three fields in order to consolidate and expedite the work. Since administration, licensing and enforcement are three principal phases of alcoholic beverage control, they were selected for survey and study in this unique undertaking.

In the hope that this report will be helpful to public officials and private citizens interested in maintaining high standards of alcoholic beverage control throughout the country, and will be of assistance to those whose duty it is to administer ABC laws, as well as to students of government, the authors respectfully dedicate their work.

TABLE OF CONTENTS

TABULAR DATA

INTRODUCTION

The precipitating cause of this study was an address by Owen J. Cleary, then Chairman of the Michigan Liquor Control Commission, at a meeting of the NABCA in Atlantic City, New Jersey in September 1947. Concisely stated, it was recommended by Mr. Cleary in that address that representatives of that Association, together with representatives of the NCSLA form a committee to explore the possibilities of drafting a model or a uniform law relating to alcoholic beverage control and to survey the operations of the various ABC agencies in the several states with a view toward establishment of uniformity in some or all aspects of their laws and regulations. It was his further suggestion that representatives of alcoholic beverage industry associations be invited to cooperate in this study.

Subsequently, preliminary discussions conducted in the fall of 1947 and during the early part of 1948, resulted in the informal establishment of this committee. Mr. Cleary and Dick R. Lane, Chairman of the Iowa Liquor Control Commission, collaborated with Walter F. Morrison, Secretary of State of the State of Colorado, and John W. Roach, Chief of the Beverage and Cigarette Tax Division of the office of the State Treasurer of the State of Wisconsin, each the ABC administrator of his own state. At that time, Mr. Lane was the President and Mr. Cleary the Vice President of the NABCA, and Mr. Morrison was the President and Mr. Roach the Executive Secretary-Treasurer of the NCSLA.

PURPOSES SET FORTH

In May, 1948, the NABCA and the NCSLA formally approved and authorized participation of their representatives as members of the joint committee. Also, in May, 1948, John F. O'Connell, Chairman of the New York State Liquor Authority, was elected President of the NCSLA and thereupon succeeded Mr. Morrison on the Joint Committee. Immediately thereafter a meeting of the Joint Committee was held, at which it was agreed to draft a proposed constitution for the committee, which was to be known as the "Joint Committee of the States to Study Alcoholic Beverage Laws." On July 8, 1948 the proposed constitution was adopted, and it sets forth the purpose of the Joint Committee in the following language:

> "To study the laws, rules, regulations and related policies of all states and the District of Columbia relative to alcoholic beverages; to make findings therefrom as to existing structures; to make recommendations, with reports to all states upon common agreement of the Committee; to prepare model laws upon agreement of the Committee; to receive contributions from organizations or governmental officials, industries or foundations, and to expend same in furtherance of the purposes herein set forth; and to take such other action consistent with the purposes enumerated herein."

On November 11, 1948 Arthur G. Burtnett, Chairman of the Alcoholic Beverages Control Commission of the State of Massachusetts, became Executive Secretary-Treasurer of the NCSLA, to fill the vacancy caused by the resignation of Mr. Roach, and thereupon succeeded the latter as a member of the Joint Committee. During April, 1949 Ray E. Tarbox, a member of the New Hampshire State Liquor Commission, filled the vacancy caused by the resignation of Mr. Lane as a member of the Joint Committee. At the present time, therefore, the Joint Committee consists of Messrs. Cleary, O'Connell, Burtnett and Tarbox. John W. Hardy, Chairman of the Virginia Alcoholic Beverage Control Board and Vice-President of the NABCA, has participated in the work of the Joint Committee since January, 1950.

NATIONAL CONFERENCE OF STATE LIQUOR ADMINISTRATORS

In the NCSLA, which was formed in Chicago in 1934, twenty-eight states and the City of Baltimore, Maryland hold membership. In these jurisdictions generally the alcoholic beverage business is conducted as a private enterprise under a system of licensing, whence arises the appellation "open license" state.

NATIONAL ALCOHOLIC BEVERAGE CONTROL ASSOCIATION

The NABCA, which was organized in 1937, represents 16 of the 17 monopoly states, within whose borders the states themselves participate in varying ways and to various degrees in the alcoholic beverage business, in addition to administering the provisions of laws and regulations, seeking otherwise to attain the objectives of alcoholic beverage control.

INDUSTRY MEMBERS

Representatives of some industry organizations accepted the invitation to collaborate with the work of the Joint Committee by making available their libraries, statistical and other reports, and such factual data and records as had been collected or compiled from time to time by their representatives, and by making financial contributions to a fund from which the expenses of the Joint Committee have been defrayed. These organizations were: Licensed Beverage Industries, Inc., the Distilled Spirits Institute, the Wine Institute, the United States Brewers Foundation, and the National Association of Alcoholic Beverage Importers, Inc. Representatives of each of these organizations worked with the Joint Committee in an advisory capacity throughout this study.

FACT FINDERS RETAINED

The Public Administration Service of Chicago, Illinois was retained to conduct a survey, which was done by analyzing the provisions of the laws and regulations of the ABC organization in each of the forty-six states and the District of Columbia, where the liquor business operates under sanction of law.

The PAS staff also collected material from various annual and other reports of ABC agencies and through the medium of a comprehensive questionnaire which was completed by thirty-five states and the District of Columbia. A more complete response to the questionnaire would have provided a better basis for evaluating the respective methods of handling administration, licensing and enforcement in the several states. Yet, the data thus collected together with the general knowledge and experience of the members of the Joint Committee, are sufficiently extensive to assist in reaching some general conclusions as to fundamentals.

In addition, members of the PAS research staff developed additional facts and obtained interpretations and suggestions from State ABC administrators and board members in some of the states as well as from various representative members of the industry. The whole range of published material on the subject of alcoholic beverage control was explored and where considered pertinent by PAS was recorded.

This phase of the work included the study and use of material assembled and published by the Wine Institute, U.S. Brewers Founda-

3

tion, Licensed Beverage Industries and the Distilled Spirits Institute. A series of tables and tabular analyses were prepared and offered by the PAS, many of which are incorporated in this report.

REPORT MADE WITH RESERVATIONS

Although care was used in the preparation of these tables and analyses, it is obvious that some ambiguities, if not errors, are included and neither the PAS nor the Joint Committee is able to guarantee their currency and accuracy. They are being used because with this reservation in mind, they are illustrative in a general way of the approaches of the several states to the problems to which the tables are pertinent. As was stated by the PAS, the material thus collected has transitory validity only since amendments are made in the ABC laws of the respective states during most legislative sessions, and since the ABC agencies themselves through changes in rules and administrative practices provide considerable fluidity in the methods of alcoholic beverage control.

HISTORY OF LIQUOR CONTROL

Although this report is being made primarily for the use of persons familiar with the history, nature and purposes of alcoholic beverage control, a statement of certain fundamental facts should be made to facilitate full understanding of the subject matter. For centuries peoples of many countries have sought to prevent or to eliminate the hazards that are privy to the unregulated manufacture, sale and distribution of alcoholic beverages.

The pages of history contain considerable evidence that the public interest requires governmental regulation of this business, and our own experience confirms the general, if not always accurate, understanding of this necessity. It is acknowledged freely by the most ardent advocates of private enterprise and by the generality of members of the alcoholic beverage industry itself. Those who comprehend the need of control and understand its philosophy find its functions in full harmony with those economic theories which support private enterprise and those which reject socialism in all its forms.

NEED FOR STRINGENT CONTROL

They know that the liquor business is *sui generis,* and that it must be considered and treated differently than every other business. The

4

principle is well established that certain anti-social conditions will inevitably flow from the operation of this business if uncontrolled by government, and that the lowest elements of society will attach themselves to it as parasites unless prevented from so doing by vigilant and resolute action by government.

The need for a system of control embodying strong and drastic measures which would operate effectively was thoroughly impressed upon legislators and others in 1933, when the Eighteenth Amendment was repealed by those who had worked long and earnestly to accomplish that objective. At the time of that historic occurrence, three centuries of experimentation in alcoholic beverage control in this country, featuring weakness, inaction, half-way measures, primary or exclusive emphasis on the collection of revenue, political connivance, judicial intrusion and delay and the abrogation of the rights of citizens to drink in moderation, had attained the status of tragic failure. Students of the situation saw that it was critically important to discover through Repeal some system of control that would promote temperance, law observance, and the public interest.

It was clear that laws with teeth should be enacted providing for sound administration and good enforcement; that well-qualified, honest persons only should be permitted to engage in the alcoholic beverage business, and that from them the law and its administration should exact strict compliance with rigid standards. It was apparent that licenses to participate in this business should be privileges only, conferring no property or other rights; that administrators of control should be independent, honest, expert and fearless, and should be given an exceptionally free hand in carrying out the will of the people in the name of their health, welfare, peace and safety.

Repeal was accomplished by the concerted action of civic-minded people who were to a large extent neither 'Wets' nor 'Drys', but who deplored the lawlessness, hypocrisy and corruption that impugned the honor, destroyed the peace and compromised the dignity of their country during the Prohibition Era. These crusaders for repeal and their supporters were not unmindful of the failures of other methods of control and the contribution to the Prohibition movement made by the sordid conditions of pre-Prohibition days.

They wanted the return of those conditions no more than they wanted Prohibition and they took steps affirmatively to prevent their return. These steps were calculated and intended to make impossible

5

the return of the saloon and its degrading influence, to prevent the "tied house" relationship between manufacturers and retailers, to forestall political corruption, and to prevent the use of the facilities of the judicial branch of government as an instrument to frustrate adequate control.

SIGNIFICANCE OF INFORMATION

It is immediately evident in a survey of this sort that majority experience is not necessarily conclusive as to best practice. Nor is it possible to determine optimum methods by examining the recent trends which frequently lead only to confusion. For example, bills proposed to the several legislative sessions during 1949 for the reorganization of administrative machinery can hardly be said to represent a trend toward improved and more efficient organization.

It was proposed in Alabama to elect the ABC Board; in California to provide for an independent five member board with ten year terms; in Connecticut to abolish the Commission and appoint a single commissioner; in Delaware, to replace the single commissioner with a three man board; in Oregon, to make the part time policy board a full time administrative board; and in Utah, to provide a five man commission selected by districts in the state.

In this connection, as in connection with all proposals to amend ABC statutes, unless the specific motivation of the author of the bill is known, it is impossible accurately to evaluate the significance of the proposals. In some instances at least, members of legislative assemblies who represent as counsel for compensation applicants or litigants before ABC agencies, are influenced peculiarly by such experience. Some such practitioners on occasions, following unsuccessful attempts to dictate, influence or ameliorate the action of the ABC agency, have proposed amendments to liquor control statutes which would seriously handicap the agency and emasculate the control system. Special interests, not infrequently to serve their own selfish purposes, have been instrumental in proposals to change, sometimes fundamentally, the provisions of control statutes.

ORGANIZATION AND ADMINISTRATION

DIFFICULTY OF MEASURING ABC EFFECTIVENESS

Students of alcoholic beverage control generally agree that no conclusion on the effectiveness of the control program can be drawn on the basis of number of enforcement actions, per capita consumption, number of outlets, amount of revenue collected or other similar isolated data. Available data seemingly indicate that there is consistently lower per capita consumption in monopoly states than in open license states, but such data do not reflect factors outside the system of control which may affect consumption, as, for example, non-resident purchasers, consumption of illegal beverages and the like. Moreover, any attempt at establishing a relationship between consumption and system of control would involve the untenable assumption that restriction on consumption as such is an objective of control.

Certainly no conclusion can be drawn regarding the effectiveness of a control program on the basis of total number of licensed premises or the number per capita or per square mile. Artificially derived indices covering, for example, such factors as the administrative costs per consumed gallon, the relationship of administrative costs to revenues derived or the relative consumption ratios of distilled spirits, wine and beer are equally unrewarding in the search for measurements either of the effectiveness or the efficiency of the control program.

SCOPE OF PAS SURVEY

It was determined when the survey was planned that it should be narrowed so as to provide an opportunity to cover some phases of operations thoroughly rather than all phases in a cursory manner. There is some doubt, viewing this decision in retrospect, of the wisdom of the choice of administration, licensing and enforcement as the specific fields of inquiry. Since, however, these were the three fields chosen for survey, separate sections of this report, each properly captioned, are devoted to those three subjects.

ADMINISTRATION

In considering the administration of ABC Laws by the individual states, it would be well at the outset to refer to the organization of the control agency itself. Principal responsibility for the administration of the ABC laws in the forty-six "control" states is assigned to fifty-two state organizational units. Forty states have one principal organizational unit and the states of Idaho, Iowa, Kansas, North Carolina, North Dakota and West Virginia have two. Thus in the forty-six states and the District of Columbia, there are fifty-three organizational units administering ABC laws.

Out of the variety of organizational structures and administrative techniques, which the several states have experienced both in alcoholic beverage control and in other regulatory and service functions, there emerge patterns which commend themselves to serious consideration. Organization is a matter of primary importance because although good organization alone does not insure good public service, yet superior and efficient public service is rarely accomplished without sound organization.

There must be present such elements as definable and appropriate objectives, capable and devoted personnel, and the application of effective techniques. It is obvious that before there can be any intelligent consideration of the type of organizational structure that the agency should possess, the functions and objectives of the agency must be defined. Although the legislators of the several states have defined the purposes of their control statutes in various terms, the principal objective of all such legislation is to protect the safety, welfare, health, peace and morals of the people of the state by fostering and promoting temperance and moderation and respect for and obedience to law. For a detailed statement of the purposes as recorded in the various control statutes, reference should be made to *Table 1*.

LOCATION OF THE ABC AGENCY IN THE STATE ORGANIZATIONAL STRUCTURE

The statutory provisions covering the composition and executive personnel of state ABC agencies are set forth fully in *Table 2*, which illustrates the widely varying ideas on this subject.

Of the fifty-three organizational units administering ABC laws, thirty-four are established as separate and independent departments. Twenty-seven of these thirty-four units are responsible for control of both beer and liquor; four (in Idaho, Iowa, Kansas and North Carolina) are responsible for control of liquor but not of beer; and in West Virginia one independent agency is responsible for control of liquor and another for control of beer. Fourteen of the fifty-three organizational units are part of the state finance, revenue, tax or treasury departments. Of these fourteen agencies, four (in Iowa, Kansas, North Carolina and North Dakota) are responsible for control of beer, whereas some other agency of the state government is responsible for control of liquor.

In most of the states in which alcoholic beverage control at the state level is vested in a state fiscal agency, licensing and enforcement are primarily functions of local government and the state's interest and responsibility are primarily in the revenue aspects. Three of the fifty-three organizational units are part of state law enforcement departments (Idaho, for beer only; North Dakota, for liquor only; and New Jersey where the Division of Alcoholic Beverage Control is part of the Department of Law and Public Safety).

The remaining two of the fifty-three organizational units are part of some other state agency; in Colorado, the Secretary of State is responsible for administering the ABC law and in Rhode Island alcoholic beverage control is assigned to the Department of Business Regulation. The organizational relationships between those administering alcoholic beverage laws and the remainder of state government may be summarized as follows:

Independent 34
Part of fiscal agency............................ 14
Part of law enforcement agency.................. 3
Part of some other agency....................... 2
                                                 ——
Total 53

Table 3 indicates that of the states replying to the questionnaire, some agency other than the ABC body in fourteen states and the District of Columbia is responsible for the collection of alcoholic beverage taxes. The degree of cooperation and joint effort between the ABC agency and the tax-collecting agency in these states varies considerably. In at least one case (Indiana), the state ABC agency has been made responsible for the administration of the state's cigarette tax laws.

9

When the several states assumed or resumed the function of alcoholic beverage control upon adoption of the Twenty-first Amendment, the creation of separate independent ABC agencies was the most common pattern and few states have altered their organizational arrangements since that time.

SINGLE ADMINISTRATOR OR COMMISSION

Of the fifty-three organizational units, twenty-two operate under the exclusive direction of a single person. In two other states (Ohio and Kansas) the ABC agencies are directed by one person, in each instance appointed by the governor, but there are, in addition, policy or review boards. In seven other states, the laws establishing boards or commissions as the principal ABC agency provide that such boards or commissions shall appoint an administrator or director (Alabama, California, Montana, Oregon, Texas and Wyoming), and the laws of Kentucky provide that the chairman of the ABC board shall be commissioner of ABC and head of the department.

Thus, out of the fifty-three organizational units administering ABC laws, thirty-two are for all practical purposes headed by one person. The remaining twenty-one agencies are administered by boards or commissions, although several of these discharge their administrative responsibilities either through the chairman or through some other executive.

RESPONSIBILITY OF THE GOVERNOR FOR ALCOHOLIC BEVERAGE CONTROL

The constitutions of most states establish the governor as the chief executive of state government and indicate that he is to be held responsible for the operation of the executive branch of state government. Through use of the appointing power, the governor is able to exercise some influence over alcoholic beverage control in all except six states, and in one of these six (Wyoming) the governor serves as one of a five member ex-officio board.

The five states in which the governor has no legal authority for or control over ABC functions are California, Colorado, Maryland, North Dakota and Wisconsin. In all of these states, however, alcoholic beverage control is entrusted to some other official elected by the people.

The governor's authority and his appointing power with relation to ABC agencies is qualified in many states by the existence of boards or commissions composed of members with fixed, overlapping terms. *Table 4* indicates the terms of the governors, the limitations on the number of terms a governor may serve for those states which have such limitations, and the number of terms of those ABC personnel who are appointed by the governor.

It is apparent from this table that the executives of the ABC agencies in very few states serve at the pleasure of, or have terms concurrent with, the governor. There are several states (Connecticut, Iowa, Nebraska, New Hampshire, Rhode Island, Texas, Vermont) in which the governor serves a two year term, whereas the ABC board or commission members serve six-year overlapping terms.

In several other states whose governors with four-year terms, with ABC commissioners are appointed to six-year terms. The appointing power of the governors is in some states further qualified by the statutory requirement that the state senate must confirm the appointments.

There are only four states in which the head of the ABC agency serves at the pleasure of the governor. These include the ABC directors in Kansas and Ohio, supervisor of liquor control in Missouri and the director of licensing in South Dakota, and of these officials the director in Kansas is the only one whose appointment is not subject to senate confirmation.

Consistent with the efforts of the various states to invest alcoholic beverage control with stability and continuity, the most common term of the ABC boards or commissions is six years. Out of the thirty-four ABC agencies which are independent organizational units, twenty-six involve appointive boards or commissions. The members of thirteen of these serve six-year terms; the members of two serve five-year terms; the members of seven serve four-year terms and the members of four serve three-year terms.

SALARIES AND SURETY BONDS OF ABC EXECUTIVE PERSONNEL

In the thirteen states in which the salary of the ABC administrator is fixed by law, as shown by *Table 2*, salaries range from $3,600 in Iowa to $16,500 in New Jersey. The mean salary of these thirteen states is $6,200.

The salaries of members of ABC boards and commissions in the states in which salaries are specified by the ABC law range from

11

Seven Dollars per diem allowance in North Carolina (except for the chairman who receives an annual salary of $6,000) and $4,000 per year for members in four states, to $15,000 per year for the Chairman of the New York State Liquor Authority. ABC board members in five of these states and the members other than the chairman in North Carolina are on a per diem basis, and their per diem payments range from Seven to Ten Dollars per day devoted to the work of the agency. Board and commission members in eighteen of the states in which one or more members are compensated on an annual salary basis receive a mean annual salary of $6,314.

In six of these states the chairman of the board receives a higher salary than the other members. The mean salary of the ABC board and commission chairman of all these states is $6,611.

A substantial number of ABC laws require that board or commission members and administrators be bonded prior to assuming the duties of their respective offices. Bond requirements for board or commission members range from $5,000 in two states (Illinois and Oregon) to $50,000 in Washington and Virginia. The most frequently occurring amount is $10,000. Bond requirements in a number of states are fixed by governors or other specified state officers. Bond requirements for administrators range from $10,000 in four states to $200,000 in Florida. The most frequently occurring amounts for administrators are $10,000 and $25,000.

INTERNAL MANAGEMENT OF THE ABC AGENCY

The ultimate success of the ABC agency depends at least in part upon the adequacy of its internal administration. Thirteen of the thirty-five states which returned questionnaries and, in addition, the District of Columbia reported that the employees of the ABC agency are subject to a civil service law. These thirteen included the more populous states of New York, Pennsylvania, Illinois, Ohio, California and Michigan, as well as the states of Alabama, Colorado, Connecticut, Minnesota, Oregon, Rhode Island and Wisconsin.

In addition, New Jersey reported that its clerical and stenographic personnel and the controller are in the classified civil service, and that the remainder who are in the "unclassified civil service" achieved tenure after three years' employment. Nebraska reported that its office personnel were subject to civil service and the District of Columbia reported that its personnel were under the Federal civil service system.

In most cases, the top administrative personnel are exempted from civil service provisions, and in some cases attorneys and hearing officers are also exempted. Missouri reported that its enforcement personnel is appointed on a "bi-partisan" basis. Most of the remaining states either depend upon informal methods to establish recruitment standards, provide a consistent pay plan, and promote uniform employment policies, or they follow an unrestricted employment policy. The questionnaire reply from Michigan included the following comment on these matters:

In Michigan, through the cooperation of the state civil service commission, qualifications for liquor law investigators have been changed and made very strict. As a result, a much higher type of individual has been brought into this field with surprisingly fine results.

Almost all the states have found that one of the most common problems encountered by state ABC agencies is the inability to recruit and keep competent personnel. Personnel problems thus encountered do not differ materially from those found in other types of law enforcement agencies. During recent years, some of the Federal, State and Municipal law enforcement agencies have developed remarkable records in integrity, effectiveness and morale, and in almost all these cases a modern system of personnel administration was the factor contributing to the improvement. The personnel systems in many states undoubtedly restrict the discretion and prerogative of the administrator or commission and have as their primary objective assurance of the continued tenure of the employee regardless of the needs or good of the service.

RELATIONSHIP WITH OTHER AGENCIES OF THE STATE GOVERNMENT

In most states legal services are provided to the ABC agency through the assignment of deputies by the State Attorney General. Although no serious objections to this practice have been registered by ABC administrators during this survey it has an inherent weakness that could have serious consequences. The successful administration of every ABC agency depends in large measure on the sound and accurate advice of counsel with regard to many of its functions.

Where its determinations are reviewed in court, the philosophy and policies of the agency as well as the pertinent and important facts of the specific cases legally interpreted are brought in sharp focus and the success or failure of the entire control program conceivably depends on the outcome. Whether the advocate who represents the ABC agency under those circumstances with ultimate responsibility to two superiors in separate and distinct departments of government can attain maximum results is questionable.

Circumstances not exactly conducive to success are easily imagined. Certainly, counsel operating within the ABC agency, responsible only to its direction has definite advantages and his performance of duty should approach more closely to the ideal. Most ABC administrators appear to feel that the status of counsel who has performed his functions ably and successfully should not be changed lightly.

The extent to which the ABC agencies make use of other common staff services of the state governments, such as those dealing with personnel and financial administration, varies considerably. This has resulted to some extent from the tendency to make the ABC agency self-sufficient and independent of these services and controls. ABC agencies, particularly in monopoly states, must perform a large share of their own purchasing, accounting and personnel administration.

RULE MAKING

The statutory provisions covering the rule making power of state ABC agencies are set forth in *Table 5*. Most states have enacted laws granting extensive power to the ABC agency to adopt and promulgate rules and regulations. In these states the power either is not limited by the ABC statute in any way or is limited only by such phrases as "not inconsistent with the spirit of this act"; "not inconsistent with this chapter"; "not inconsistent with any of the provisions of any statute of this state"; and "not inconsistent with law."

The statutes of several states provide that the rules and regulations promulgated as above have the force and effect of law. Several of these states enumerate by statute specific subjects for rule making in addition to the general authority given above. In these cases there is usually a statement to the effect that the delineation of certain specific subjects for rules does not in any way affect the over-all power to promulgate rules and regulations.

Such sweeping rule making powers are not specifically granted by law in the remaining states. The statutes of North Dakota do not confer any rule making power, and the statutes of South Carolina presumably limit rule making to specific subjects. The Illinois law provides that the Liquor Control Commission may "recommend to local commissioners rules and regulations not inconsistent with law," and also:

To fix by regulation the standards of manufacture of alcoholic liquors not inconsistent with Federal laws *** and to establish rules not inconsistent with Federal laws for the proper labeling of containers or barrels, casks or other bulk containers or bottles of alcoholic liquor manufactured or sold in the State (Sec. 108, Chap. 43, Ill. Rev. Stat.). The Illinois Commission reports that regulations covering labeling have been adopted but that standards of manufacture have not been the subject of regulation.

The New Mexico law does not specifically confer rule making power but does require the distribution of "all rules and regulations established and promulgated under the provisions of this act."

The New York State Liquor Authority does not have general rule making powers. It is, however, empowered to adopt rules governing manufacture of alcoholic beverages, disciplinary procedures, bonds of licensees, labeling, signs and other specific subjects. New York reports that the phases of control which have been the subject of rule most frequently are:

1. The fixing of closing hours by local ABC boards, and
2. The fixing of moratoria during which local ABC boards are prohibited from accepting applications for licenses of various types.

The Federal law governing alcoholic beverage control in the District of Columbia confers rule making power on the district commissioners rather than on the ABC board. The rule making powers of some states are circumscribed by the limitations on general powers granted to the ABC agency. In Iowa, for example, the rule making power of the Liquor Control Commission does not extend to beer. Rule making power generally represents one of the most striking examples of the variety of operations among the ABC agencies of the several states.

Such power has been delegated to control agencies because the legislatures themselves cannot be expected to and should not specify in detail the manner and method of administering the substantive provisions of the law. For example, the amount of discretion which is appropriate for the administrative agency cannot be set forth

15

precisely by definition, but the legislature can preserve and protect its function, which indeed it cannot delegate, to make laws by establishing certain specific standards and guideposts with which the administrative agency must conform in establishing and promulgating its rules.

In most states it appears that a rule becomes effective upon adoption by the ABC agency without hearing, publication or other formality. In other states, for example, Michigan, California, Ohio and Minnesota, the rule making processes conform to, or are governed by, standard administrative procedures acts. Michigan, for example, reports the following steps which are required before a regulation becomes effective:

1. Approval of the Attorney General
2. Adoption by the Liquor Control Commission
3. Signature of the Governor which gives it immediate effect in case of emergency or compelling extraordinary circumstance.
4. Filing of the original and two duplicate copies in the office of the Secretary of State together with fifteen mimeographed copies for the Legislative Committee, or if the Legislature is in session, a copy for each member. Those rules which are not given immediate effect by the Governor becomes effective when published in the Supplement to the Michigan Administrative Code.

The rule making processes in Ohio and California are governed by these states' administrative procedures acts which, among other things, requires public notice and hearing prior to the time a rule becomes effective. The Minnesota statute provides for a public hearing on proposed rules after "30 days written notice to registered trade representatives." Connecticut reports the following provision in connection with its rule making process:

After adoption by the Commission new regulations must be referred to the Attorney General for approval and then printed in the Connecticut Law Journal. They are then referred to the next session of the General Assembly. They become effective when printed in the Law Journal, but the General Assembly may revoke them.

A number of states provide for advance notice of a proposed rule and opportunity for protest; only a few states, however, in addition

16

to those mentioned, make a public hearing on a proposed rule mandatory.

Almost all states make some effort to make copies of new rules available to licensees or to other parties affected, although the methods used by respective states vary considerably. *Table 6* shows the methods reported by the thirty-five states and the District of Columbia which replied to the questionnaire.

ADMINISTRATIVE HEARINGS

The provisions of ABC statutes of the respective states regarding administrative hearings are summarized in *Table 7*. As indicated in a footnote this table is intended only to portray the types and variety of legal provisions involved. Absence of an entry for a particular state does not mean necessarily, for example, that the ABC agency of that state does not hold such hearings.

These hearings vary greatly as to degree of formality depending, firstly, on the subject matter of the hearing and, secondly, on the state involved. For purposes of clarity and understanding it should be observed that administrative hearings may be broken down into two general categories, namely:

1. those concerned with the issuance of licenses, and
2. those involving disciplinary proceedings to revoke, cancel or suspend licenses.

Several states provide for "hearing officers" who conduct the original hearings both on licensing and on disciplinary matters, and who report their findings to the commissioner, commission or board. Many states make administrative provisions for hearings even where not specifically required to do so by law. For example, New York reports that:

As a matter of *law*, an applicant who, within ten days after notice by local ABC board that his application has been recommended for disapproval, requests in writing a hearing thereon is entitled to such hearing before the Liquor Authority. As a matter of *policy*, the Liquor Authority also holds hearings on all applications for license where (a) premises for which license is sought are not currently licensed; (b) protests against favorable action on the application have been filed either with the Local Board or with the Liquor Authority; (c) a change in type of license

17

is sought (as, for example, from a license authorizing sale of beer to a license authorizing sale of liquor and wine as well); and (d) in all other instances where in the opinion of the Licensing Board there is reason to set up a hearing.

Table 7 indicates that among the states there is a wide variety of legal provisions governing hearings.

In many states there is no requirement, for example, that the decisions of the agency be set forth in writing, supported by a statement of the reasons on which the determination was based. The extent and nature of statutory provisions for administrative procedure are such as to suggest that there is little uniformity within the states between ABC administrative procedures and those of other regulatory state agencies.

To some extent this condition results from the fact that an ABC license confers a privilege only and not a right, and reflects the thinking of legislators that it is against public interest to vest any property right in an alcoholic beverage license. For these reasons the alcoholic beverage business is distinguished and differentiated from other lawful businesses.

Administrative hearings on license applications should be broken down as follows:

(a) Hearings of an original character to assist the ABC agency to determine whether the applicant is qualified and his premises is suitable;

(b) Hearings to review in an appellate capacity the action of some other agency of government approving or disapproving an application for a license; and

(c) Hearings to review the action of another branch of the ABC agency itself approving or disapproving such application.

In general, greater formality is accorded hearings in proceedings to discipline licensees than is to be found in hearings on applications. As to the former, at least, and to a lesser extent to hearings on applications for a license the following normal, procedural steps appear to be observed generally, in many instances without statutory mandate:

1. All parties are notified of hearing by mail
2. All parties may be represented by counsel
3. Hearings are open to the public
4. Presentation of briefs is permitted but is not required

5. Rules of evidence are not strictly observed
6. Cross-examination of witnesses is permitted
7. A record of proceedings is kept

JUDICIAL REVIEW

As shown by *Table 7*, the determinations of ABC agencies are reviewable by courts of law and equity in many states. These reviews fall into two principal categories, which may be described as:

1. Review by *certiorari*, and
2. Review by trial *de novo*

In an action of *certiorari*, the court confines its review to the record of the subject matter as kept by the ABC agency and restricts itself to consideration of the question whether the agency in reaching its determination acted within the law. This type of review is intended to keep from the courts the mass of litigation which is likely to occur where review is on the merits and to vest in the ABC agency both the authority and the responsibility for the maintenance of effective control. Where the law is respected, the court does not substitute its judgment for that of the ABC agency in this type of review but sustains the agency's determination if supported by substantial evidence.

The court may affirm the decision of the ABC agency, may remand the matter for further proceedings, or it may reverse or modify the decision if substantial rights of the petitioner have been prejudiced because the action of the agency was arbitrary or capricious, or (1) in violation of constitutional provisions; (2) in excess of statutory authority; (3) based on unlawful procedure or otherwise affected by error of law; or (4) unsupported by substantial evidence as shown by the entire record as submitted.

Table 7 reflects that certiorari and de novo are each used in the same number (13) of the states and that some other states use one or the other method as to certain restricted classes of determinations.

Review by trial *de novo* has the characteristics of an original hearing and requires the exercise of judgment by a court not only on the law but on the merits as well. This type of review discounts the value of the experience, technical competence and specialized knowledge of the ABC agency and substitutes the opinion of a court, which may be wholly uninformed as to alcoholic beverage control, for the opinion of persons expert in the field of alcoholic beverage control.

19

PROBLEMS POSED BY JUDICIAL REVIEW

The experiences of the Pennsylvania Liquor Control Board furnish an insight into the problem of attaining proper standards of ABC administration and enforcement in jurisdictions where determinations of the ABC agency are reviewable by the courts by trial *de novo.* Up to 1937 the sole power to suspend or revoke licenses in Pennsylvania reposed in the courts. In the first Annual Report of the Pennsylvania Liquor Control Board to the Governor, the Chairman, a former Superior Court Judge, reported that sentences imposed by the courts were "varied and not in strict conformity with the penalty clauses of the Liquor Control Act."

Apparently dissatisfied with the results, the Legislature granted this authority to the Liquor Control Board, but in a sense there has been judicial nullification of this grant. As reported by Mr. M. Nelson McGeary, Professor of Political Science of the Pennsylvania State College, in his work entitled *Pennsylvania and the Liquor Business,* Professor McGeary made the following observations:

> *About one-third of the applicants for all types of licenses, who are turned down by the board, carry an appeal to the courts. The judges, consistently over a period of years, have ordered licenses issued in at least two out of three of such cases appealed. The Board likewise runs into trouble with the courts when it suspends or revokes licenses * * *. About one out of every fifteen persons whose licenses are suspended by the Board appeals to the courts. This figure possibly would be higher if compromise payments in lieu of suspension were not so readily procurable. Over a period of years the Board has been fully sustained by the courts in only about one-third of the appeals cases. If the Board is not reversed completely, the suspension often is reduced. Appeals are taken more readily by persons whose licenses are revoked by the Board; in most years as many as three out of four such licensees ask the courts to overrule the Board. The Board is sustained on the average only about half the time. In 1945, however, when three-fourths of all revokees went to the courts, the judges overruled the Board in 81% of the cases. It should be noted that the number of appeals to the courts varies widely from county to county. In some areas appeals are rare; in others, they are encouraged because of the consistent reversals of the Board.*

20

In this same work, Professor McGeary drew the following conclusions:

1. No state agency in Pennsylvania is faced with problems any more difficult than those of the Liquor Control Board.

2. The reversals of orders of the Board have been too numerous to encourage high administrative morale.

3. It would appear desirable to seek a more uniform enforcement of the liquor laws throughout the state.

4. In its disputes with the courts the Board generally was in the position of advocating the stricter interpretation and enforcement of the alcoholic beverage laws.

5. In some counties the courts are prone to interfere to such an extent that effective liquor control by the Board is seriously impeded. In many other counties, however, the Board has received consistent support from the courts.

6. The Liquor Control Board should not be unduly restrained by the courts in its day to day activities ***. The courts should also serve as a valuable watchdog to overrule Board actions which are arbitrary or are manifestly unjust or unlawful. But in the case where the Board has arrived at a decision after careful procedure and on the basis of substantial evidence, a judge should not substitute his opinion for that of the Board.

Another student of the Pennsylvania system has also commented upon the workings of control in that Commonwealth. Based on his study as Executive Director and Counsel of Pennsylvania Alcoholic Beverage Study, Inc., over a period of many years, Mr. Randolph W. Childs in his book entitled *Making Repeal Work* made the following comment regarding licensing by the courts which he described as "particularly liable to abuse":

"To place responsibility for granting liquor licenses upon judges lowers the prestige of the bench. It was painfully proved, prior to the era of national prohibition, that judging and licensing make a dangerous mixture. The old maxim 'sober as a judge' was no guarantee that politics could be kept out of liquor licensing. When licensing has been a judicial privilege or responsibility, it has been rumored too frequently that attorneys with friends in high places could obtain licenses for their clients and that they charged scandalous fees to use this alleged influence with the courts."

It is Mr. Child's recommendation that a system of judicial appeal should meet two fundamental requirements, which he expressed in the following language:

(1) A licensee who has made a heavy investment on the basis of a liquor license should not have his license suspended or revoked by the arbitrary or unlawful action of an administrative body.

(2) On the other hand, where the administrative agency has made a ·decision, which is supported by substantial evidence and which is in accordance with law, a court should not substitute its own judgment for that of the agency, either as to whether the law has been violated or as to what penalty should be imposed.

One of the important phases of judicial review of the determinations of ABC agencies covers the matter of so-called stays by which the courts postpone the effective date of the agency's action. Postponement, procrastination and delay in judicial determination spelled the doom of many efforts to maintain good order, law observance and decency in the alcoholic beverage business before Prohibition. Experience shows that the majority of those seeking such stays, especially the serious malefactors, do so primarily to prolong the life of their license and not with any real hope of ultimate success in keeping that license.

During the period of such stays in those cases, the sanctions on the operations of the business are tremendously weakened and the disposition to operate in an abandoned manner is strong and prevalent. In this field the old adage "Justice delayed is justice denied" is particularly applicable. Every agency of government possessed of responsibilities involving alcoholic beverage control, whether it be in the legislative, executive or judicial branch, should perform its duties faithfully and should cooperate to the end that violations may be terminated promptly and that sanctions may be applied expeditiously.

The administration of an ideal law (which has never been written) by an ideal ABC agency (which never existed) could be subverted, weakened and nullified by judicial handling involving long stays except for the soundest of reasons or short stays for weak or no reasons. The practice of issuing such stays liberally appears to be progressing; it constitutes a creeping paralysis threatening the health and vigor of the most robust ABC administrations.

LICENSING

Licensing is one of the two principal methods by which the objectives of alcoholic beverage control are attained; the other being enforcement. The licensing function is performed to restrict participation in the alcoholic beverage business to honest, able and qualified business people, and to prevent the intrusion therein of anti-social, marginal and otherwise unqualified operators. The extent of the alcoholic beverage licensing functions of the various states is indicated by the following tabulation of the number of retail licenses issued during the last completed fiscal year by the states returning questionnaires.

OPEN LICENSE STATES

Arkansas	3,309	Nebraska	3,340
California	40,817	Nevada	1,500**
Colorado	3,424	New Jersey	12,345
Connecticut	7,726	New Mexico	1,019*
Delaware	495	New York	61,152
Florida	12,627	North Dakota	2,463
Georgia	7,564*	Rhode Island	2,003
Illinois	24,535	South Carolina	10,419
Indiana	6,998	South Dakota	2,838
Kentucky	3,853*	Wisconsin	29,776
Minnesota	18,153	District of Columbia	1,991
Missouri	12,080		

MONOPOLY STATES

Alabama	3,076	Oregon	5,367
Idaho	2,946	Pennsylvania	21,070
Iowa	6,000**	Vermont	1,795
Michigan	27,707	Virginia	7,696
New Hampshire	2,287	Washington	5,082
North Carolina	15,018	West Virginia	5,507
Ohio	38,926		

23

The number of retail outlets reported by the Licensed Beverage Industries in 1946*** for those states which did not return questionnaires is as follows:

Open License States

Arizona	1,534	Maryland	5,456
Kansas	2,500	Massachusetts	8,966
Louisiana	13,390	Tennessee	4,905
	Texas	14,606	

Monopoly States

Maine	2,077	Utah	1,165
Montana	1,700	Wyoming	465

RESPONSIBILITY FOR LICENSE ISSUANCE

With respect to licensing functions, there are three schools of thought which may be summarized as follows:

(a) The state should have exclusive control of licensing.

(b) The local subdivision of the state should have this control exclusively.

(c) Control as to this function should be the joint responsibility of the state and the local subdivision.

The agency or agencies responsible for the issuance of retail licenses (and, incidentally, for the disciplinary action against holders of such licenses) are shown for each state in *Table 8*.

Ultimate state control of the licensing function predominates in considerably more instances than does local control. Slightly more than fifty per cent of the states have seen fit to retain virtually complete authority for all retail license issuance or to retain at least that degree of control necessary to insure that the specific approval of state authorities is obtained before retail alcoholic beverage outlets may begin operations. The laws of the following states assign primary licensing authority for the retail sale of alcoholic beverages to the state agency:

---

* Questionnaire incomplete; number is estimated or computed from collateral sources.
** Estimate made by state ABC agency.
*** *Beverage Distilling Industry Facts and Figures, 1934-1945.* The number of retail outlets for any particular state is somewhat smaller than the number of licenses issued, since many outlets require more than one kind of license.

Open License States	*Monopoly States*
Arkansas (liquor and wine)	Idaho (on-sale liquor)
California	Michigan (off-sale licenses)
Connecticut	Montana
Delaware	New Hampshire
Kansas (liquor)	Ohio
Kentucky	Oregon
Louisiana	Pennsylvania
Missouri	Utah
Nebraska	Vermont (on-sale liquor)
North Dakota (beer)	Virginia
South Carolina	Washington
Texas	West Virginia

The Michigan statutes provide that licenses for on-sale beverages may be issued following approval by local authorities, and the Michigan agency reports that, even though not required to do so by law, off-sale licenses must also receive local approval as a matter of practice.

The laws of Oregon provide that the state licensing authority may require the local governmental authorities to submit recommendations relative to a proposed license, and the laws of California, Washington and Kansas require that notification of license applications be sent to local authorities, who may file objections. In Nebraska applications for on-sale liquor licenses in municipalities must be submitted through the municipal authorities for their recommendations. Some of the other states also seek, as a matter of practice, recommendations of local authorities before licenses are issued.

In addition, local authorities are authorized to issue supplementary licenses in the following of the states listed above: Arkansas (liquor), Idaho (on-sale liquor), Kentucky, Louisiana, Missouri, Montana, North Dakota (beer), Texas, Utah, Virginia, and West Virginia. In each of these cases the states have retained primary licensing authority but have provided that local authorities may issue supplementary licenses.

LOCAL LICENSING POWER

The extent of this local licensing power varies. City or county authorities in Montana, for example, are given only the privilege of issuing licenses and, so far as is indicated in the law, may not regulate or prohibit except as to the collection of the license permit fee. Local authorities in Louisiana and Missouri may, on the other hand, pass ordinances providing not only for the issuance of local licenses and the collection of fees, but also for accompanying regulatory controls with respect to such matters as zoning and hours of operation. Such additional controls are normally authorized so long as they do not conflict with the state ABC laws or impose upon applicants unreasonable licensing requirements.

Other states in which there are both local and state participation in the licensing process may be divided roughly into seven categories, as follows:

1. *State authority issues after reviewing recommendations of local ABC board*: (In New York half of the members of the local ABC boards are appointed by local authorities and half are appointed by the State Liquor Authority. Three of the four members on each of the local Indiana boards are appointed by local authorities, and the remaining member is appointed by the state ABC commission.)

Open License States	*Monopoly States*
Indiana	None
New York	

2. *State authority issues after reviewing recommendations of local authorities; local authorities may issue supplementary licenses*:

Open License States	*Monopoly States*
Arizona	None
New Mexico	

3. *State authority issues following approval by local authorities*:

Open License State	*Monopoly States*
South Dakota	Maine
	Michigan (on-sale licenses)

4. *State authority issues following approval by local authorities; local authorities may issue supplementary licenses*:

Open License State	*Monopoly State*
Tennessee (off-sale liquor)	Alabama

26

5. *Local authorities issue following approval by state authority*:

Open License States	*Monopoly State*
Massachusetts	Vermont (wine and beer)
Minnesota (off-sale liquor)	

6. *County authority issues joint state-county license on approval of state authority; municipalities may issue supplementary licenses*:

Open License State	*Monopoly States*
Florida	None

7. *Both state and local authorities issue; licenses must be obtained from each*:

Open License States	*Monopoly States*
Arkansas (beer and light wine)	Idaho (beer)
Colorado	Iowa
Georgia	North Carolina
Illinois	
North Dakota (liquor)	
Tennessee (beer)	

In many of the states listed under Item 7 above, principal and in some cases final jurisdiction over license issuance rests with the local unit. In Illinois, for example, the state cannot refuse to issue a license when a local license has been obtained; in Iowa the required state license is issued by the State Tax Commission for purposes of collecting revenue, and not by the Iowa ABC agency; in Georgia the application for a state license must be accompanied by a city or county license; and, in Idaho, counties have final authority with respect to beer licenses.

In the following states license issuance is a primary responsibility of the local jurisdiction:

Open License States	*Monopoly State*
Kansas (beer)	Wyoming
Maryland	
Massachusetts	
Minnesota (on-sale liquor)	
Nevada	
New Jersey	
Rhode Island	
Wisconsin	

27

In the District of Columbia the exclusive responsibility for license issuance belongs to the ABC Board.

In most of these states, licenses may be issued only in accordance with state regulations, and in some cases (notably New Jersey and Rhode Island) licenses are subject to review by the state authorities. The local issuing authorities in the majority of these states are the legislative bodies of the cities, towns, or counties having jurisdiction over the premises to be licensed. The laws of some states delegate the function to special local issuing authorities. In Massachusetts, for example, licenses for premises in most cities are issued by special licensing boards appointed by the mayors and subject to the confirmation of the boards of aldermen or city councils, and only after approval by the state ABC commission.

Neither *Table 8* nor any of the discussion with reference thereto attempts to cover all the respective state provisions for the issuance of train, boat, airplane, or other special types of retail licenses, although normally the issuance of licenses of these types is the responsibility of the state.

In Iowa there is exclusive local control over the issuance of beer licenses for sales by the drink. In Illinois final responsibility for the granting of retail licenses is vested in local authorities, and in Wisconsin local governing bodies have complete jurisdiction over retail licensing. In Minnesota the state has authority over licenses permitting sale at retail for off-premises consumption, but such authority as to licenses permitting sale for consumption on the premises is vested in the municipalities.

LIMITATION OF NUMBER OF LICENSES TO BE ISSUED

Table 9 summarizes the statutory provisions of the several states relative to limitation of the number of alcoholic beverage licenses which may be issued. It indicates those authorities responsible for determining the number of licenses it may issue in any particular area. It outlines the provisions of those arbitrary, numerical limitations on license issuance set forth in the laws of certain of the states.

The laws of 10 open license and 6 monopoly states contain no provision pertaining to the numerical limitation of licenses.

In eight open license and five monopoly states and the District of Columbia, discretion for determining the number of licenses to be issued is specifically vested in the authorities responsible for the

28

issuance of alcoholic beverage licenses. Certain subjective criteria for the determination of desirable limitations on the number of licenses are set forth in the laws of a majority of these states. These laws require, for example, that the issuing authorities shall take into consideration such factors as public convenience and advantage, public interest, or the reasonable demand of the public. Or, issuing authorities may be directed to apply limitations on the basis of the character of the population, the nature of the locality, or the number of licenses already in effect.

The laws of three open license states and one monopoly state vest responsibility for determining the number of licenses to be issued in local governmental authorities. In all but one case these local authorities are the respective legislative bodies of the cities, towns, or counties. Maryland law assigns responsibility for this determination to special city or county boards of license commissioners.

Arbitrary numerical limitations set by law govern the number of licenses to be issued in 10 open license and 5 monopoly states. There is considerable variation in the actual limitative provisions of these laws, but in most instances they state the maximum number of licenses which may be granted in particular geographical areas or political subdivisions per specified population increment.

Nearly two-thirds of the states, it appears, have refrained from placing in their laws arbitrary numerical limitations on license issuance and have left this determination to their respective licensing authorities. The laws of approximately half of these states remain silent on license limitation, thus placing the issuing authorities in position to utilize objective measurement of the qualifications of persons and premises as the prime limiting device. The subjective criteria set forth in the laws of the other half still leave the issuing authorities free to make use of objective means of determining whether or not licenses should be issued.

LIMITATION DOES NOT ALWAYS LIMIT

There is little evidence that limitation imposing by law arbitrary numerical limitations on the number of licenses that may be issued result in a substantially fewer outlets for the state. This is due in some instances to the fact that the number of existing outlets existed when the limitation was imposed. *Table 10* shows the number of retail outlets per 1,000 population retailing any type of alcoholic

29

beverages, first for those states which have numerical restrictions in their laws, and then for those states that either make no mention of license limitation or give state or local authorities discretion in this matter.

The mean number of outlets per 1,000 for open license and monopoly states combined is shown in the center column of the table. This table is imperfect in that it does not take into account variations caused by restrictions on classes of license, the extent to which limitations were exceeded when limitations laws were enacted, and changes in population. It is somewhat significant that, contrary to what might be expected, there is but a slight difference in the number of retail outlets per 1,000 population between those states whose laws arbitrarily limit the number of licenses and those which do not. A slightly larger number of outlets per 1,000 population is in fact found in those states which have included numerical limitation in their liquor control legislation.

It is significant that apparently in no state in which the law vests discretion to limit the number of licenses in the licensing authority has such agency adopted an over-all numerical limit. Questionnaire replies from four states in which discretion is vested in the state authority provide fairly typical reactions as to the use of such discretion:

New Hampshire. "Although this Commission could exercise discretionary power as to the number of licenses to be issued, this is seldom invoked."

New York. "In connection with the fixing of the number of licenses to restaurants which will permit them to sell alcoholic beverages for consumption on the premises, the criterion used is: Is the premise for which the application is filed in operation as a bona fide restaurant? In connection with the limitation of package store licenses which permit the holders thereof to sell alcoholic beverages for consumption off the premises, the criterion is: Will the issuance of the license applied for serve public convenience and advantage?"

New Mexico. "The Chief of Division is vested with such authority. The criteria used are the number of licenses outstanding in a given locality, the population of the locality, and peculiar circumstances affecting the locality such as whether it is a resort community, industrial, close to Indian reservations, the difficulties

30

of enforcement because of remoteness, and generally public need and demand."

Oregon. "The Liquor Control Law does not indicate to the Commission the number of licenses to be issued. This matter is based entirely on the discretion of the Commission as to necessity, based on public convenience. In addition to insuring that the applicant and the premises are properly qualified under the law, the Commission is obligated to insure that there is a need for the license applied for from the standpoint of public convenience or necessity. This factor is being consistently checked upon by field representatives of the Commission and, if there is any question for a need of additional licenses of any type at a given location, a special study is made of the area in question."

CRITERIA FOR THE SELECTION OF PERSONS TO BE LICENSED

Table 11 shows the frequency of occurrence in the ABC laws of the various states and the District of Columbia of thirteen basic criteria for use in determining the qualifications of applicants for retail ABC licenses. This must be read and understood in the light of the fact that in the exercise of the discretion vested in them by law many of the control agencies as a matter of practice and policy require applicants to meet some or all of these thirteen standards, even when they are not mentioned in the law itself.

The states are listed alphabetically in the first column. Each of the following numbered columns corresponds to one of the numbered criteria listed at the foot of the summary table. An "X" in a numbered column opposite the name of a state indicates that the alcoholic beverage laws of the state require that a license applicant be eligible with respect to that particular criterion. The total column at the right side of the table shows the total number of these important standards which each particular state has included in its ABC laws. The vertical column totals show the number of states which have incorporated each particular standard in their laws.

As in virtually every other area of alcoholic beverage control there is a striking lack of uniformity in the laws of the various states with respect to these basic requirements. The objective measurement of all license applicants against most or all these thirteen guideposts would be of inestimable value in measuring qualifications of applicants. Only two states (Kansas and New Hampshire) have seen fit to incorporate as many as seven of these criteria in their ABC laws, and only seven others (Connecticut, Delaware, Florida, Illinois, New Jersey, New York, and Wyoming) have incorporated six. Three states (Georgia, Nevada, and Virginia) have included only one in their laws.

The licensing requirements most frequently set forth in the ABC laws of the various states are those with respect to United States citizenship (39 states and the District of Columbia), clear record in respect to violation of ABC laws (29 states and the D. of C.), and in respect to conviction for a felony (28 states and the D. of C.), residents within the state (25 states), good repute and moral character (24 states and the D. of C.), and of specified minimum age (21 states and the D. of C.).

Only four states have included in their laws requirements that applicants be financially responsible or that applicants not use alcoholic beverages to excess. Five states by their ABC laws specifically require that the individual be a legitimate party in the interest. No state requires by law that applicants be able to read and write or that they demonstrate any understanding of the ABC laws and rules under which they must operate.

The issuing authorities of most states have had assigned to them by law or have assumed discretion in imposing qualifying conditions in addition to those specifically set forth by law. The laws of Virginia, for example, contain only one of the criteria listed in *Table 11;* the Virginia Board, however, reports that it employs additional criteria:

> The Board considers each application on its merits, being especially concerned as to the suitability of person and place . . . the general policy of the Board is not to grant a license to a person who is not a citizen of the United States or who cannot read or write the English language; also to limit on-premise beer licenses to establishments serving some food, at least sandwiches, and on-premise wine licenses to bona fide restaurants serving regular meals.

LITERACY REQUIREMENTS

A number of states report that they have imposed, by rule, the additional qualification that the applicant must be able to read and write the English language. Michigan is the only state that reported that the applicant "must pass a written examination based upon the State Liquor Law and Rules and Regulations of the Commission."

MINIMUM QUALIFICATIONS

There appears to be considerable variance among the states as to the amount of discretion vested in the ABC agency to establish minimum qualifications of applicants when such discretion is not specifically vested in the agency by law. Vermont, for example, reports that:

> The attorney general has ruled that the Liquor Control Board has the discretionary power to refuse to issue a license even though the applicant meets all minimum qualifications if the Board finds, in the exercise of its sound judgment and discretion, that the issuance of a license to the applicant in question will be injurious to the public health, safety, or morale.

The opposite extreme is probably represented by the states of Alabama, Idaho, and New Mexico, which report as follows:

> *Alabama.* "All persons are entitled to a license except those outlined in Section 24 and 28 of Title 29, Code of Alabama, 1940."
> *Idaho.* "Every person who qualifies for a license is entitled to one."
> *New Mexico.* "The qualifications for licenses are prescribed by statute and the Chief of Division (of Liquor Control) has no discretion in the matter."

CRITERIA FOR USE IN SELECTING PREMISES TO BE LICENSED

Table 12 shows the frequency of occurrence in the ABC laws of the various states and the District of Columbia of certain factors which bear upon the suitability of premises for licensing. As in the case of licensing criteria utilized in determining the eligibility of individuals for licenses, the standards applicable to premises are subject to considerable variation, and, although the laws of few states have utilized many of these to achieve maximum objectivity in the licensing of premises, yet the control agencies in exercising their discretion frequently use some of them even where they are not mentioned in the control statutes.

An "X" in the table opposite the name of any state indicates that the laws of that state require that premises be eligible with respect to the particular criterion shown at the head of the column and the column totals show the number of states which have incorporated each into their laws.

DISTANCE BETWEEN LICENSED OUTLETS

Most states have included in their laws or regulations standards with respect to the minimum distance between licensed outlets, on the one hand, and various public and private institutions or other outlets, on the other. Thirty-one of these states have specified minimum distances from schools, twenty-five have specified minimum distances from churches, eight have specified minimum distances from hospitals or other public institutions; and three have specified minimum distances from other licensed retail alcoholic beverage outlets.

ZONING REGULATIONS

Eleven states and the District of Columbia specifically provide by law that licensed premises may be located only in those areas not prohibited to them under local zoning ordinances. The laws of nineteen states provide that premises to be licensed must be open to view from outside or from the entrance. Eleven states prohibit openings from premises to be licensed into other rooms, connecting buildings, or living quarters.

Several additional qualifications regarding the premises to be licensed are imposed by the rules and regulations or by the operating practices of the licensing authorities of a majority of the states. New York, which incidentally conducts one of the most thorough investigations of premises to be licensed, reports that examinations are made into:

> . . . the history of the premises for which the license is sought and such facts with reference thereto as bear upon its reputation, the character, reputation, and responsibility of the landlord; the type of neighborhood, and the physical set-up of the premises, with emphasis upon the space, equipment, and facilities for the operation of the proposed business.

A property file is maintained by the New York State Liquor Authority containing rather complete information on each premise licensed by the state, including interior and exterior photographs, record of ownership, record of licenses granted, and reports of violations.

34

The license application and/or investigational reports forms of several states in which the state is the licensing authority indicate that some attention is given to various other physical features of the premises to be licensed, including:

1. General sanitary condition and sanitary facilities.
2. Structural condition of the building and compliance with building, plumbing, and electrical codes.
3. Seating capacity, number and accessibility of exits, use of combustible furnishings, and other factors affecting the degree of fire hazard.
4. Other uses made of the same structure, with particular reference to living or lodging quarters, storage, or fire-hazardous uses.

The extent to which unfavorable reports on these various features contribute to license denials varies considerably from state to state and, generally, in the absence of specific provisions in the law or minimum criteria.in the rules and regulations, the discretion of the issuing authority in each particular case governs.

STEPS IN THE LICENSE ISSUING PROCESS

The sequence of events involved in the issuance of a license in the respective states generally conforms to a natural pattern of application, investigation, consideration, and issuance or denial, but there is a variety of emphasis and methods used in the successive steps.

INSTRUCTION FOR APPLICANTS

Almost all states have made copies of their ABC laws available in printed pamphlet form, and many states have made the rules and regulations of the ABC agencies similarly available. Very few states, however, have prepared informational materials directed specifically to license applicants or licensees. Some notable exceptions are:

1. A comprehensive question-and-answer type pamphlet which Michigan makes available to license applicants.
2. A series of handbooks (one for each class of licensee) prepared by the Pennsylvania Liquor Control Board and providing information on "Licensees: How Procured—Privileges Granted—Obligations Involved."

35

3. "The Retailer's Handbook" issued by the Liquor Control Administration, Department of Business Regulation, State of Rhode Island and Providence Plantations.
4. A printed pamphlet entitled "Instructions to Applicants," is made available by the New York State Liquor Authority to all applicants.

PUBLIC NOTICE OF APPLICATION

Table 13 indicates the requirements of the several states with respect to public notices in cases of alcoholic beverage license applications. The laws and regulations of twenty-five states and the District of Columbia provide that public notice of pending retail license applications be given either through publication in newspapers or through posting on the premises and in other places. In only two of the twenty-five states (Michigan and South Dakota) is the publication restricted to certain types of licenses. All others require such public notice regardless of the type of retail license for which application is being made. The laws of the remainder of the states fail to make specific provision for such public notice, and presumably no state has imposed a notice requirement when such is not required by law.

HOLDING OF HEARINGS ON LICENSE APPLICATIONS

In the laws and practices of the several states it is difficult to make a clear distinction between hearings which are held prior to any formal action on a license application and those which are more in the nature of appeals or protests after original action on an application has taken place. *Table 14* indicates the general practices of several states regarding hearings, as reported by questionnaire, and also indicates the volume of hearing actions of those states for the most recent fiscal year.

Requirements that hearings be held prior to the granting of retail liquor licenses are found in the laws and regulations of twenty-five states and the District of Columbia. These hearings are held for the presentation of protests and the obtaining of information with respect to the qualifications of individuals and premises for licensing. They are separate from, and are not to be confused with, those hearings which take place following appeals of the decisions of licensing authorities to appeal boards and courts.

In all but four of the states providing for compulsory hearings, the hearings are held in all licensing actions regardless of the type of license applied for or whether or not a hearing is requested by any of those concerned. Hearings are authorized or the holding of hearings is implied in the laws of several states but are not specifically required. In the remaining instances the laws and regulations make no mention of such hearings.

The laws and regulations of twenty states and the District of Columbia specifically provide that written or oral objections and protestations of interested persons, including property owners, representatives of churches and private institutions, and various public officials, be taken into consideration prior to the issuance of retail alcoholic beverage licenses. Such objections may be presented during public hearings, to individual licensing officials, or to appropriate commissions or boards at their regular meetings. As in the case of hearings and investigations there are a number of less formalized methods whereby licensing officials are made aware of protests against license issuance.

TIME LIMITS FOR ACTION ON APPLICATIONS

In several states minimum and maximum time limits for approval or disapproval of license applications are imposed by law or, in a few cases, by administrative regulations. The states that reported such time limits in their questionnaire replies are as follows:

Alabama. No time limits except that, on renewals, licensee must apply 60 days before expiration of existing license and Board must notify licensee within 30 days of application receipt if objection raised.

Arkansas. Minimum 15 days on liquor licenses—no maximum. Minimum 10 days on beer licenses—no maximum. No minimum or maximum on wine licenses.

California. Minimum of 15 days from notice to local officials and posting premises. No maximum.

Colorado. Must approve or disapprove within 15 days after filing.

Connecticut. Applications are held 3 weeks from first publication notice during which 10 residents can file remonstrance.

Kentucky. No limitation, except that Board may be mandamused by Circuit Court for failure to act on a license application.

Nebraska. No action taken for 15 days before hearing. No maximum limitation.

New Jersey. Minimum—2 days following last publication of notice. No maximum beyond "reasonable time."

37

New York. Decision of State Liquor Authority or local ABC board must be rendered within 30 days of application or hearing.

Ohio. Minimum 15 days after application, except renewal. No maximum.

Washington. Minimum—10 days from date of notice to local authorities.

Wisconsin. Must be on file 15 days prior to grant. Must be granted within 2 months.

LICENSE TRANSFERS, REMOVALS AND RENEWALS

Table 15 lists the statutory provisions of the several states regarding the procedures for license renewals and transfers.

Table 16 indicates the presence or absence in the laws of the several states of four specific provisions relating to the transfer and removal of licenses. A dash opposite the name of any state indicates that the state ABC law does not specifically cover the subject under the particular column heading. Entries in the first column relative to license transfers do not take into account license transfers to executors or administrators in the event of the decease of licensees. Thus, where provisions for license transfers apply only to such transfers, no entry will appear.

Six states permit neither license transfer from person to person nor removal from one premises to another. In these states changes in ownership or location can be effected only through applications for completely new licenses in accordance with the regular new-license application procedures. Nine states and the District of Columbia provide for both transfers and removals but specify in their laws that each shall be subject to the same basic requirements as original applications. Two other states which provide for both require that transfers be in accordance with initial license application requirements but fail to provide similarly specific restrictions in the case of removals.

Four states permit the transfer of licenses without specifically providing in their laws that such transfers shall be subject to the same provisions as would apply to original applications. Similarly, thirteen states permitting removals have omitted the requirement in their ABC laws that such removals meet initial application standards. In many of these states, however, the licensee is required either by formal regulation or administrative practice to meet standards equal to those established for an original applicant.

38

In seven states both transfers and removals are authorized, but only in the discretion, and following the consent, of the various licensing authorities. In none of these seven cases do the laws specifically require that the transfer or removal be in accordance with new license requirements.

A number of states provide special forms to effect a transfer or removal and a few states impose a fee to cover the same. Also, in those states in which the licensing authority is decentralized to local jurisdictions, some of these jurisdictions may have imposed restrictions on license transfer and removal similar to those contained in some of the laws of other states.

License renewal constitutes an extremely important phase of alcoholic beverage control. Licensing authorities who are authorized and equipped to examine each renewal application virtually as though it were an application for a new license are in a position to anticipate and prevent countless enforcement problems which might later arise.

Table 17 indicates the extent to which ABC laws deal with specific phases of the renewal process. As indicated in the column of the table referring to the term of licenses, all of the forty-six states with ABC laws and the District of Columbia grant retail liquor licenses for a period of one year. This means that each licensee and his premises must receive the approval of licensing authorities annually.

The advantages to be gained from annual renewal are to a large extent nullified, however, when all licenses expire on the same date. In thirty-seven states and in the District of Columbia, such mass expiration of retail ABC licenses is the rule. As of a certain date, licensing authorities in the majority of these states must grant or refuse to grant thousands of licenses on the basis of such information as is submitted with the renewal applications.

Ten states have provided that all or at least a substantial portion of the retail licenses are to expire on different dates. In most of these states licenses are valid for one year from the date of issue. Renewal applications are, therefore, submitted throughout the year, thus giving the licensing authorities an opportunity to examine more thoroughly the qualifications of applicants and premises for continued operation. In three of these ten states, Minnesota, Pennsylvania, and New York licenses in particular districts or municipalities expire on the same date, but expiration dates are not the same throughout the state.

Licensing authorities have a much better opportunity to investigate renewals if it is required that applications be submitted well in advance of the expiration dates. Advance filing of renewal applications eases, to some degree, the burden on the licensing authorities, particularly in those states whose laws specify one statewide expiration date. Eleven states require advance filing from five to sixty days prior to expiration.

Four of these eleven states combine this advance application with staggered expiration dates, thus allowing licensing authorities to examine the renewal applications in advance and throughout the year. The laws of twelve states provide that renewals are subject to the same qualifications both as to persons and premises as are initial license applications. In practice, many other states doubtless apply these same standards in the case of renewals.

ENFORCEMENT

A clear and specific definition of the assignments of authority and responsibility among agencies and individuals concerned is essential to any undertaking. As the complexity of the undertaking increases, so too does the need for clear-cut delegation. State ABC programs are for the most part quite complex and normally require large scale participation by both state and local authorities. It is surprising, therefore, to note that delegation of responsibility for enforcement is frequently omitted from the state ABC laws, or is made in such general terms that only forced and projected interpretations can fix responsibility.

This condition is further confused by the fact that enforcement of ABC laws is a two-fold operation following separate and distinct channels. In the first place, ABC laws are penal in character in that violations of their provisions are defined either as felonies or misdemeanors, prosecutions for which must follow the usual forms and channels adopted by the respective states for the prosecution of all crime. This type of enforcement utilizes the services of peace officers, juries, prosecutors, criminal courts and penal institutions.

ADMINISTRATIVE ENFORCEMENT

The other phase of enforcement is administrative in character and utilizes the services of persons who are not ABC personnel only as witnesses. Through this channel disciplinary actions are taken against licenses and permits. However, regardless of the specific approach of any state toward the fixing of the respective responsibilities of the regularly established law enforcement agencies and the personnel of the control agencies, it is apparent that both criminal enforcement and administrative enforcement are dependent in large measure upon the active, intelligent and prompt performance of duty by local law enforcement officers. Most states seek to obtain good enforcement through the fullest use of both methods.

RESPONSIBILITY FOR ABC LAW ENFORCEMENT

The ABC laws of nineteen states and the District of Columbia, as indicated under the first column of *Table 18*, contain no specific state-

41

ment of the assignment of the basic or ultimate responsibility for ABC enforcement, although in some of these states there are statements assigning responsibility for some phase of the enforcement process, such as detecting violations, prosecuting violators and the like. In the majority of these nineteen states, the respective ABC agencies are made responsible for general administration of the ABC laws, and in some instances are authorized to enact regulations relating to enforcement.

So far as specific delegation of basic or ultimate enforcement responsibility is concerned, however, the laws are either silent or inconclusive. The ABC laws of twenty-seven states make reasonably specific delegation of basic responsibility for enforcement. In twelve of these states, basic enforcement responsibility is vested in the respective state ABC agencies. The Nebraska ABC Law, for example, states:

> It is intended by this grant of power to adopt rules and regulations with the commission clothed with broad discretionary powers to govern the traffic in alcoholic liquors and to enforce strictly all the provisions of this act.

New Hampshire ABC Law also vests basic enforcement responsibility in the state ABC agency thus:

> The primary responsibility for the enforcement of all liquor and beverage laws shall be upon the commission.

In fourteen more of these twenty-seven states the ABC laws vest basic enforcement responsibility in both the state ABC agency or its personnel, and in local governmental or law enforcement authorities. Utah's ABC law provides:

> All inspectors appointed under this Act, and all sheriffs, deputy sheriffs, mayors, city judges, justices of the peace, constables, marshals and peace officers, and all district, county, city and town attorneys, and clerks of courts shall diligently enforce the provisions of the Act.

Similarly, North Dakota's ABC law states:

> The Attorney General, his inspectors and all peace officers in the State of North Dakota shall be charged with the duty of diligently enforcing the provisions of this act and all other provisions of law relating to the manufacture and sale of beer, alcohol or alcoholic beverages.

Finally, of the twenty-seven states which fix enforcement responsibility by specific statutory provision the laws of the State of one (Iowa) vest such responsibility in local authorities.

FIXING OF ENFORCEMENT RESPONSIBILITY

Table 18 also shows on a state-by-state basis the location of responsibility for each of four significant phases of ABC law enforcement including: (1) detection of violations of state ABC laws, (2) prosecution of ABC violators, (3) suspension or revocation of ABC licenses, and (4) hearing of appeals or review of decisions relative to ABC license suspensions or revocations.

LOCATION OF RESPONSIBILITY FOR DETECTION
OF VIOLATIONS

As indicated in *Table 18* the laws of forty-one states directly or indirectly vest responsibility for detecting violations of state ABC laws in both state and local enforcement authorities. In most of these states local law enforcement authorities are made responsible for detecting violations in their respective jurisdictions and are directed to assist state enforcement officers in their investigative activities. Four states (Arizona, Kentucky, Missouri and Pennsylvania) have vested responsibility for detecting violations in the state ABC agency or other state law enforcement agencies, and, apparently, have not provided specifically for the participation of local authorities.

The ABC law of one state (Iowa) delegates responsibility for investigation and detection to various local authorities without giving comparable responsibility to state agencies. The great majority of the state laws, however, provide for the sharing by state and local authorities of responsibility for detecting ABC violations.

LOCATION OF RESPONSIBILITY FOR PROSECUTING
VIOLATORS

The ABC laws of twenty-two states have no specific provisions as to the location of responsibility for the prosecution of ABC violators, although in these states such responsibility, insofar as it relates to criminal prosecution, inferentially rests upon public prosecutors and to the extent that it is administrative in character is probably the responsibility of the ABC agency.

Fourteen state ABC laws make both state and local officers responsible for instituting prosecution and in seven states officers of the liquor control agency or other state officers are responsible for ABC law prosecutions. Finally, in three states, the responsibility is vested in local officers, usually district or local prosecuting attorneys.

LOCATION OF RESPONSIBILITY FOR DISCIPLINARY ACTION

Suspension or revocation of ABC licenses as penalty for non-compliance with ABC laws and regulations or other applicable statutory and regulatory provisions constitute the most effective method of ABC enforcement. Responsibility for the actual suspension or revocation of ABC licenses is in some instances vested in the same authorities as are basically responsible for ABC law enforcement and for license issuance.

In twenty-seven states the authority to suspend or revoke licenses is vested solely in the respective state ABC authorities or other state officials. In two of these states (Michigan and Nevada) the state authorities revoke upon the request or recommendation of local authorities. Revocation authority is vested in both state and local authorities in seventeen states.

In Iowa only local authorities are given responsibility for license revocations and in Kansas the State Director of Alcoholic Beverage Control is responsible for liquor license suspensions and revocations while the respective local licensing authorities are responsible for suspensions and revocations of non-intoxicating malt beverage licenses.

THE ROLE OF LOCAL LAW ENFORCEMENT AUTHORITIES

As indicated in *Table 18,* virtually all state ABC laws vest at least some enforcement responsibility in the various peace officers of cities, towns and counties. Because local enforcement personnel generally play such an important role, it is important that they be well-trained, properly directed and schooled in all phases of ABC enforcement. Upon them and their work prosecuting attorneys and ABC agencies depend largely for criminal and administrative enforcement.

Table 19 is designed to show the methods used by various state ABC agencies for instructing personnel of local law enforcement agencies in ABC enforcement practices and for evaluating the effectiveness of local ABC enforcement activities. Entries are based on information from questionnaires submitted by thirty-five states and the District of Columbia.

44

INSTRUCTIONAL PAMPHLETS AND GUIDEBOOKS

Only eight of the states replying to the questionnaires indicate that their ABC agencies have prepared and issued special instructional pamphlets or guidebooks for use by local enforcement authorities. A majority of state ABC agencies distribute copies of the ABC laws and/or regulations, but these do not even purport to take the place of publications designed especially for the use of those who must enforce the ABC laws.

TRAINING COURSES

Training courses conducted by state ABC agencies for the purpose of acquainting local law enforcement personnel with proper enforcement practices and procedures where used, have been found valuable. Only six of the thirty-five states reporting, plus the District of Columbia, now conduct such courses.

SYSTEMATIC VISITS

State ABC personnel in eighteen of the states reporting make systematic visits to local jurisdictions to confer with local law enforcement officials on ABC enforcement at the local level. Uniform and well-coordinated state-wide enforcement programs to a substantial degree have been aided by the establishment of close working relationships between the state and local authorities. Regular contacts with local officers by state ABC personnel have been found to promote uniform enforcement standards state-wide. Without such contacts state ABC agencies have met difficulties in determining the quality of local enforcement work and in identifying problem areas.

INFORMATIONAL RELEASES

Thirteen state ABC administrators indicated that their agencies prepare and distribute special informational releases for the use of local enforcement authorities and that such releases have contributed a great deal to effective statewide enforcement programs. They have been used for: (1) informing local police units of revisions in state ABC laws and regulations, (2) explaining new and improved enforcement techniques and procedures, (3) pointing out problem areas in the over-all enforcement program, and (4) commending effective enforcement work in certain areas and pointing out deficiencies in others.

New York reports that it has sought to insure effective enforcement "through a broad public relations program which has aimed at clarifying the responsibility of local communities for the enforcement of the ABC law in the minds of the police, press and public.'' The state ABC agency in New Jersey also makes effective use of the press in calling attention to the paramount importance of stringent local enforcement.

OTHER METHODS OF PROMOTING LOCAL ENFORCEMENT ACTIVITY

In a number of states all or a part of the proceeds of license fees collected by the states are distributed to the local governmental units of the place of origin of the fees. In Michigan, and perhaps in a few other states, the state ABC agency by implication has the power to withhold these funds in cases where no enforcement effort is shown.

POLICE POWERS OF STATE ABC ENFORCEMENT OFFICERS

Table 20 summarizes information relative to certain police powers conferred on state ABC enforcement officers as reported in questionnaire replies. Adequate enforcement, in the opinion of some ABC agencies, requires the delegation of normal police powers to ABC enforcement officers and agents and where such delegation is not provided for by law, some feel that ABC enforcement personnel are severely handicapped in carrying out their duties.

Other ABC agencies feel that there are sufficient peace officers duly constituted and paid as such to handle all phases of the enforcement program to the extent that the powers of arrest, search and seizure are involved. As the table indicates, twenty-five of the states replying have conferred upon their personnel the power of arrest.

Most states, either by law or by rule, have provided that, as a condition of the license, ABC agents have the right of inspection of the licensed premises at any time or at least at such times as the premises are open for business. The ABC laws of five states (Florida, Indiana, Maryland, South Dakota and Utah) specifically require that the right of entry, search and seizure on licensed premises shall be consented to by applicants as a condition of the license.

LICENSEE RECORDS AS AN AID TO ENFORCEMENT

In order that enforcement personnel may have an effective means of checking activities in the alcoholic beverage trade, it is essential that licensees be required to keep proper records of consignments, inventories and transactions such as purchases and sales. As indicated in *Table 21,* a substantial majority of the state ABC laws provide that

46

such records must be kept. Seventeen states require all four trade groups, manufacturers, transporters, wholesalers, and retailers to maintain specified records or to submit to the ABC authorities equivalent information in the form of periodic reports. Fourteen other states require that all but transporters maintain records or submit reports.

Fewer than half of the state ABC laws, however, require either the keeping of records or the submission of reports by transporters of alcoholic beverages. This is accounted for to a large degree by the fact that only a few states license transportation companies making deliveries into or transporting alcoholic beverages from place to place within the states. Some ABC administrators feel that complete control calls for the coverage of those engaged in transporting these beverages as well as those engaged in manufacturing, wholesaling, and retailing thereof.

STATE ABC ENFORCEMENT STAFFS AND ACTIVITIES

Table 22 summarizes certain information relative to state ABC enforcement personnel and activities as recorded in the questionnaires returned by thirty-five states and the District of Columbia. The tabulated material reveals considerable variations among the states with respect to both staffs and enforcement activities.

The number of enforcement personnel in the state ABC agencies varies from none in Iowa and Nevada where local authorities have primary enforcement responsibilities, three in Arkansas and six in North Dakota, to 275 in California and 340 in Pennsylvania, reflecting extensive state participation in ABC enforcement activities in these latter two states.

In a number of the states in which state enforcement units are very limited administrators generally feel that they cannot properly enforce the ABC laws or coordinate local enforcement activities without increases in enforcement personnel. Some of the comments from state administrators in answer to the question: "In your opinion, what modifications in the law, available funds, or methods would contribute to the more effective enforcement of alcoholic beverage control laws in your state?" are significant in this regard:

Arkansas (3 enforcement officers)—"Funds for investigators."

New Mexico (7 enforcement officers)—"The greatest handicap to the adequate enforcement of the laws at the present time is the lack of sufficient funds to employ proper personnel."

47

Delaware (10 enforcement officers)—"Enlarge the enforcement force."

Colorado (10 enforcement officers)—"More enforcement officers."

Nebraska (17 enforcement officers)—"Very meager funds are available in Nebraska for this type of work. With sufficient funds it could be very much improved."

Approximately half of the states replying to the questionnaire reported that the state police or traffic patrols participated directly in the enforcement of ABC laws. In many of the other states the state police or traffic patrols frequently assist in special cases, but are not generally available for day-to-day enforcement activities.

The number of license revocations by state ABC agencies during the last completed fiscal year for the states replying to the questionnaire varied from none in 7 states and 1 in 4 more, to 183 in Ohio, 101 in Virginia, and 98 in South Carolina. New York reported that 258 licenses were involuntarily terminated after formal hearings, 198 by cancellation and 60 by revocation. In each instance, the license was destroyed but revocation carried with it an added property disqualifying as a matter of law the holder of such license from entering this business for a period of at least two years.

Suspensions by state ABC agencies in the same period varied from none in 9 states and 10 in Alabama and Delaware, to 759 in Pennsylvania, 618 in California, and 326 in Missouri. The number of arrests for ABC violations made by state ABC agencies ranged from none in 4 states, 8 in Colorado and 10 in North Dakota, to 4,028 in Alabama, 2,485 in Georgia, 2,354 in Virginia, and 937 in Ohio.

Violations of ABC laws referred by state ABC agencies to prosecuting officers for court trial varied from none in 4 states and the District of Columbia, 8 in Colorado, and 10 in North Dakota, to 2,485 in Georgia, 2,026 in Virginia and 1,304 in Indiana.

There are a number of factors which to some extent account for the wide variations in volume of enforcement actions summarized in *Table 22*. One such factor is the point of emphasis of enforcement activities. A number of states, for example revoked only a few ABC licenses during the last completed fiscal year, but suspended a substantial number, or, conversely, revoked many licenses and suspended only a few. In these and other comparable cases it appears that the enforcement agencies tended to place emphasis on those enforcement methods facilitated by legal provisions and prevailing practices.

Another significant factor influencing variation in activity statistics is the matter of distribution of enforcement responsibility between state and local units. A small number of arrests by state ABC agents may in some cases be accounted for by the fact that local enforcement officers, either because of specific legal requirements or as a matter of practice, make virtually all arrests for ABC violations. A large number of arrests by state ABC agents may, on the other hand, indicate that local law enforcement officers leave ABC enforcement matters largely to state ABC officers.

Finally, the enforcement procedure prescribed by statute or followed as a matter of practice is apt to cause enforcement statistics variations. A good example may be found with respect to arrest and prosecution statistics for Georgia. In the last completed fiscal year, 2,485 arrests were made for ABC violations and 2,485 ABC violation cases were referred by state ABC agencies to prosecuting authorities. These two figures are the same probably by virtue of the procedure of referring automatically all arrest cases to prosecuting authorities.

FEDERAL-STATE COOPERATION

The maintenance of close and cooperative relationships between state and federal authorities can do much to facilitate effective ABC enforcement at the state level. The work of the U. S. Treasury Department, particularly the Alcohol Tax Unit, is important to state ABC agencies since certain areas of enforcement are common to both the state and federal organizations. The ATU is responsible for the administration of a range of federal laws relating to the alcoholic beverage trade.

Among other things the unit is charged with the determination and assessment of taxes and penalties on liquors, the inquiry and investigation into the filing of returns for occupational and commodity taxes, the chemical analysis of liquors and in a restricted way the regulation of distilled spirits, wines and malt beverages moving in interstate commerce. Thus, whenever state and federal authorities can work together in these and other enforcement areas the state enforcement arms are, in effect, supplemented by whatever personnel the federal agency brings to bear on a particular activity.

ABC administrators in a large number of the states reporting indicate that relationships with the ATU are satisfactory and that a close degree of cooperation is maintained. The questionnaire returned from Indiana, for example, contained the comment that:

The cooperation with this department by the Federal Alcoholic Tax Unit has been entirely satisfactory in every instance. Since the inception of the Alcoholic Beverage Commission of Indiana in 1935, there has been no instance where complete cooperation between the two departments has not been given. In many instances, the departments have worked with such complete coordination that the two departments operated almost as a single unit.

The questionnaire reply from California also indicates that cooperation with the ATU is satisfactory:

In no manner could the Federal Alcohol Tax Unit more effectively cooperate with our liquor enforcement division of the State. We have worked effectively and cooperatively together for many years, and I feel safe in saying we enjoy each others' full confidence. I believe California is an outstanding example of cooperation between the Federal and State agencies dealing with liquor control.

COOPERATION BETWEEN STATE AND FEDERAL AGENCIES NEEDED

Several state ABC administrators in their replies to the questionnaire indicated a number of areas in which they believed that state-federal working relationships in ABC enforcement problems might be improved. Following are the comments of two state ABC officials with respect to this matter:

Michigan—If Federal laws were changed to make it mandatory that no retail liquor dealers' or wholesale dealers' tax stamps would be issued by the Internal Revenue Department without their first having obtained a state license to sell alcoholic beverages, this would curb the illegal activity in sales decidedly.

Missouri—The Federal Alcohol Tax Unit could cooperate with state officials by seeking an amendment to the Federal laws whereby the Federal tax stamps would not be issued promiscuously to individuals regardless of their qualifications to be engaged in the liquor business. The Alcohol Tax Unit could cooperate by giving tax stamps only to persons duly qualified and licensed by the state liquor agency.

In connection with the proposal that the issuance of federal stamps be made contingent upon the procurement of a state license, it should be noted that the ATU reportedly will make available to the state ABC agency a list of all purchasers of the federal stamps.

The questionnaire returned by New York contained the suggestions that the ATU could cooperate more effectively with state officials by:

1. "Indicating to all applicants for federal permits the requirements of the state in respect to being licensed.
2. "Referring to state ABC agencies all information pertaining to violations of the state laws of which the Alcohol Tax Unit has knowledge.
3. "Reporting to state ABC agencies the names and addresses of licensees found guilty of refilling bottles."

In a number of states possession of federal stamps is prima-facie evidence of the possession of alcoholic beverages for sale. In this connection the Arkansas Supreme Court recently ruled that possession of federal tax stamps was grounds for such an assumption. At the time of the decision it was disclosed that the state of Arkansas had issued 593 retail liquor licenses and that the Federal Government had issued 1,021 tax stamps for retail liquor outlets. (Taken from *The Journal of Commerce,* New York, April 1, 1949).

ABC officials in three southern states indicated on questionnaire replies the need for closer state-federal working relationships and for a greater number of federal enforcement personnel. Their answers to the question: "In what manner could the Federal Alcohol Tax Unit more effectively cooperate with state officials in the enforcement of alcoholic beverage control laws?" were:

Alabama—"By increasing personnel and giving more assistance in apprehending violators bringing unstamped whiskey into this state from other states for re-sale."

Florida—"By a closer working arrangement for mutual cooperation, especially in connection with moonshine activities."

Virginia—"By having more Federal agents."

INDUSTRY'S PLACE IN ENFORCEMENT

In all programs of enforcement of ABC laws and regulations, the role of members of the alcoholic beverage industry is indispensable. Indeed, despite all the differences among the states in the use of various enforcement techniques, there is a virtual unanimity of opinion of all students and administrators of control that licensees are truly the shock troops of enforcement. Certain it is that in the field of prevention licensees have a unique function, the significance of

51

which is well illustrated by the maxim that ''an ounce of prevention is worth a pound of cure.''

The licensee who knows and respects his business supervises its operations with a firm hand. He makes logical plans and takes prudent precautions to prevent violations on his licensed premises. He anticipates infringement on good order, forestalls trouble, and takes summary action should misconduct or disorder develop. He must be understanding, alert, active and forceful. In short, he must be at once a good business man, a good psychologist, and a good policeman. The importance of the enforcement role of the industry, particularly as to premises licensed to sell alcoholic beverages by the drink can neither be over-estimated nor over-emphasized.

There is a school of thought which assumes for or assigns to one branch of the industry the right and duty of enforcing some provisions of the law by industry action against offending members of some other branch. Such enforcement may be effected, for example, through such devices as denial to a retail licensee of alcoholic beverages by supplying distributors. There is no gainsaying the effectiveness of such summary action but it has some rather obvious shortcomings.

In the first place, it involves a usurpation of functions of government by private interests which reflects unfavorably both on the industry and on government. Again, it subjects enforcing industry members and groups to hazards involving both civil and criminal liability. Furthermore, industry members generally lack the experience, independence and detachment required to insure enforcement which will command industry and public respect.

There is another school of thought which adheres to the position that each licensee should be charged by law with the positive duty to police his own employees and his own premises, and that as to all other industry members his contributions to enforcement should consist of good example and moral suasion. Proponents of this philosophy feel that no greater offering to good enforcement can be made by industry members, and they evaluate highly the contributions of individual licensees already made through those channels. They also rate highly the good work in this field already done through practice and promotion by many industry members, some of whom operate through industry organizations and others independently, but they believe that in this, as in other phases of enforcement of ABC laws and regulations, potential accomplishment has not been approached.

SUMMARY AND CONCLUSIONS

Early in the work of the PAS it became evident to the Joint Committee that in the three fields of liquor control to which the PAS survey was specifically restricted (Administration, Licensing and Enforcement) there were these three theoretical possibilities of an affirmative character: (1) a model law; (2) uniformity in statutory and regulatory provisions; (3) standardization of the operation of the ABC agencies through alignment of statutory, regulatory and policy activities with certain basic fundamental principles.

Shortly thereafter it was agreed that for the present the idea of drafting a model law should be abandoned. Since ABC statutes to be effective must be in substantial conformity with public thinking and, since the opinions and attitudes of citizens of the several states now differ, conflict and clash with such vigor and determination, a model ABC law at the present time as a practical matter is a contradiction in terms.

Efforts to crystallize the results of the work of the PAS so as to deduce from the data thus collected provisions for uniform laws, have demonstrated that with no more data than are now available to the Joint Committee it would be necessary too frequently to substitute theory for critical examination of the operations of the control organizations of the individual states. Likewise, too frequent resort to theoretical conclusions in lieu of a comprehensive and definitive understanding of the strong and weak points of the individual systems and agencies would be required. Unless and until a complete examination and analytical survey of the activities of each control agency has been made on the scene of its own operations, it would appear premature to formulate proposals to enact uniform laws.

The present study relates to ABC agencies exclusively and would, therefore, appear to deal with the same problems in each state, but this fact must be considered in the light of the additional fact that each state has its own peculiar forms of legal procedure and differs from other states in respect to its judicial precedents, legislative approaches to the administrative process, and methods of providing the checks and balances that are inherent in the application of the doctrine of the separation of the powers of government.

It would be possible at this time on the basis of information before us to compare the organizational and administrative set-up of each state as reflected in the tabular analyses in this report with a theoretical ideal, the outline and features of which could be gleaned from textbooks on administrative practices generally and from such studies as have culminated in the "Model State Administrative Procedure Act" and the "Federal Administrative Procedure Act."

This, however, would be a hazardous approach which might well result in mischief, since some systems which appear on paper to vary widely from the textbook ideal actually may operate so as to accomplish effective control while maintaining high standards of fairness and objectivity. Experimentation which would seek to attain uniformity among the states as, for example, in the conduct of hearings on matters relating to liquor control, would seem to be premature and unsound since reform of administrative practices within individual states should be more comprehensive and general. Furthermore, such uniformity among the states conceivably could be accomplished through the destruction of uniformity within the states—truly an anomalous accomplishment.

Our position at the present time is in substantial conformity with that set forth as the policy of the National Conference of Commissioners on uniform state laws by its president, Mr. William A. Schnader. Mr. Schnader stated the determination of that Conference "to recommend for uniform adoption a greatly diminished number of acts and to decline to make the recommendation that any act be uniformly adopted unless there is real reason why the law of all states ought to be the same on the subject matter with which the act deals." (Reported in the Annual Report of the American Bar Association, 63rd Annual Meeting, held at Philadelphia, Pa., Sept. 9-13, 1940.)

Our study, observations and experience convince us that as to the third theoretical possibility we have reached the position where we can recommend an affirmative approach. We believe that standardization of the operations of alcoholic beverage control can be promoted conservatively and effectively by alignment of statutory, regulatory and policy activities with the following important basic principles:

PRINCIPLES TO BE USED AS GUIDEPOSTS TO STANDARDIZED CONTROL

1—To be effective as to acts that are *mala prohibita,* penal statutes including ABC laws must have the approval of the people and must be in substantial conformity with public thinking.

Comment:

This is not to imply that the validity of law depends upon its popular acceptance or that penal statutes are not necessary and desirable when large numbers or groups of people subject thereto are not in agreement with their provisions. The special, indispensable need of ABC laws for support of this kind is well illustrated by the failure of the Eighteenth Amendment and the statutes implementing its provisions, which furnish an excellent example of the results of enactments in this field of which the people generally disapprove and by which in large number they refuse to be bound. If public thinking is erroneous, all media of public education should make their respective and proper contributions to correct that condition.

2—Control of the operations of the alcoholic beverage business aims primarily at the prevention of certain socially undesirable conditions, which history and experience have demonstrated, will develop in the absence of such control.

Comment:

This principle is given expression in the preambles and enacting clauses of the control laws of the several states, where the purpose of the law has been stated in such language as "promoting temperance and moderation", "preventing intoxication", "preventing the return of the old-time saloon and the evils thereof", and "for the protection of the safety, welfare, health, peace and morals of the people." The history of this country, including colonial days, records legislative efforts with widely varying provisions, all showing acceptance by citizens of the necessity of control of this business by government.

3—Primary responsibility for the control of the alcoholic beverage business belongs to the individual states:

Comment:

Such investment is provided for specifically by the Twenty-First Amendment, by virtue of which each state has full authority to determine just what is needed in the way of regulation to protect the health, welfare, safety and morals of its people. Exclusive federal control does not permit adequate adjustment of the control system to accommodate the many regional and sectional customs and attitudes. Whether it is advisable for the state to delegate to its communities participation in that control and, if so, the

55

extent of such local participation, are moot questions. If local participation is provided, great effort must be exerted to insure the appointment of administrators who are strong, independent, and able to stand out against the corroding as well as corrupting influences of the political pressures which, at this level, are particularly virulent and dangerous.

4—Alcoholic beverage control should be commensurate with its purposes and should provide the control agency with sufficient power, authority, funds and facilities to enable it to assure accomplishment of those purposes with latitude for uncertainties.

Comment:

This principle has been well-stated in the enacting clauses of many of the control statutes in such language as "this entire act shall be deemed an exercise of the police power of the state for the protection of the welfare, health, peace, temperance, and safety of the people of the state and all its provisions shall be liberally construed for the accomplishment of that purpose." (From the Texas Liquor Control Law.) Such power and authority must be complemented by responsibility identical in kind and degree, in order that the public may know where responsibility truly rests and may be guided accordingly.

5—The collection of revenue from the alcoholic beverage business must be considered and treated as a subordinate interest of government and the control by the state of the alcoholic beverage business to prevent socially undesirable conditions must always prevail over revenue considerations.

Comment:

Despite the fact that an increased volume of business by this industry would produce greater revenue for the state, such increase is undesirable if incompatible with control objectives. Similarly, increases in the amount of taxes levied on alcoholic beverages are inconsistent with control objectives if they tend to increase the illegal participation in the manufacture, transportation, distribution and sale thereof.

6—Effective administration of control is most likely to result from a system in which the ABC agency is a separate and distinct unit of government.

Comment:

Such status is not, however, an indispensable condition of good control which has been and can be attained where ABC functions are integrated with existing departments. We feel that good control is possible under such conditions, provided that there is a line of responsibility from the head of the ABC agency directly to the governor.

7—The ultimate success of the state ABC agency depends at least in part upon the adequacy of internal administration, and sound principles of public administration should be applied to the governmental control of alcoholic beverages.

Comment:

The application of such principles is as essential to effective alcoholic beverage control as to every other function of government. Where civil service is a recognized state function and the authority of the ABC agency as to personnel is thereby limited, there should be close correlation of the functions of the two agencies to the end that inefficiency or uselessness of service may not exist. Just and fair treatment of personnel are needed, on the one hand, to insure good morale, and on the other courtesy to the public, respect for authority and devotion to duty on the part of all personnel must also be forthcoming.

8—Alcoholic beverage control has been and can be administered satisfactorily by an ABC agency headed either by an individual, be he commissioner or executive director, or by a board or commission.

Comment:

Advantages and disadvantages exist in both systems. In theory, where there is one person at the head of the agency, greater efficiency, expedition and consistency are to be found. On the other hand, theoretically at least, greater capacity and broader vision are to be expected from a board, and the public is inclined to the belief that greater justice and equity flow from board action. We have found good examples of excellent administration under both systems.

9—Stability and continuity in the personnel of the control agencies are of the utmost importance to good control.

Comment:

One of the most glaring weaknesses which exist in the field of alcoholic beverage control is to be found in the frequent turnover among ABC administrators. This condition is the result largely of changes of the chief executives of the states, but is also influenced, in many instances, by inadequate compensation and all too frequently by unhealthy political pressure. Good alcoholic beverage control requires administration by an organization expert in this field. Practice cannot justify this theory where changes in key personnel occur with undue frequency.

10—Responsibility for performance of the two principal functions of control, namely, licensing and administrative enforcement, should be vested in the same agency of government.

Comment:

Where one agency has either power without the other, its ability to insure high standards among licenses is definitely curtailed. Whether the agency responsible for licensing and enforcement should administer the program of collecting taxes on alcoholic beverages is a moot question. If the responsibility for such collection is so joined, care must be taken to treat as the paramount concern of government the prevention and elimination of social evils and not the collection of revenue. It is well established in theory and practice, however, that there should be close cooperation and teamwork among all agencies of government responsible for the performance of these various functions.

11—The enforcement of the criminal provisions of ABC laws should be the responsibility of all law enforcement officers.

Comment:

Traditionally, in most if not all states, all peace officers and prosecuting attorneys are responsible for the prevention and suppression of crime and the prosecution of criminals. Since control statutes generally contain provisions classifying violations thereof either as felonies or misdemeanors, the enforcement of such provisions should be handled in the same manner as is that of other penal statutes, that is, they should be enforced by all peace officers and prosecuting attorneys. Whether the detection and prosecution of these violations, to the extent that they are criminal in character, should also be the responsibility of the control agency and, if so the extent of such responsibility, are moot questions. Administrative enforcement through disciplinary action against licenses and permits must be provided for and it must be neither contingent nor conditioned upon criminal conviction. The sanctions provided by criminal prosecution alone have never sufficed to "protect the safety, welfare, health, peace and morals of the people" in connection with the operations of the alcoholic beverage business, nor have they accomplished a degree of compliance essential to the attainment of that common objective of control.

Where local law enforcement agencies fail culpably to perform their duties of enforcement, the state itself should take over the enforcement program in such manner as is consistent with the laws of the particular state.

12—The ABC statute should fix the respective responsibility of the various agencies of government relating to the enforcement of the ABC law.

Comment:

Since state ABC programs are generally complex and normally require large scale participation by both state and local authorities, it is highly important that the respective responsibilities of each agency be definitely fixed in order that each may understand clearly its own obligations and that it may know the functions of the other involved agencies. Unless this action is taken, confusion, misunderstanding, avoidance of responsibility, and conflict in performance of duty, are likely to occur, all of which are injurious to good control. Enforcement responsibility if positively centered is most likely to succeed. Unless it is a separate function delegated to a specific agency exclusively, ABC enforcement instruction should be part of the program of training law enforcement officers charged with general responsibilities. Even under such specific delegation the agency responsible for enforcement should work in close cooperation with other law enforcement agencies of general jurisdiction.

13—Constant evaluation and stimulation of enforcement activities through training those charged with the responsibility and through regularized inspectional supervision tend to promote good ABC enforcement by contributing to good morale, proper efficiency, and over-all uniformity.

Comment:

Inspectional service should seek to determine not only whether routines are being followed but whether they adequately accomplish the purposes intended. Such services may sample public opinion to determine the worth of existing routines. Among techniques which have been found helpful in promoting good enforcement are the following:

(a) Regular meetings of enforcement officials.
(b) Distribution and use of guide books, instructional pamphlets, and informational bulletins.
(c) Use of regular reports from enforcement officials to those responsible for criminal and administrative enforcement.
(d) Occasional meetings between enforcement officials and licensees.
(e) Occasional public meetings to promote constructive criticism and informed comment.

14—Authorization to participate in the alcoholic beverage business is a privilege subject to control in the public interest.

Comment:

A license or permit to participate in this business should not confer any right or privilege other than as specified in the ABC law. Any statute which undertakes to create a property right in the terms of such license is inimical to and destructive of the public interest. To obtain a license, the applicant must prove his qualifications and to retain it he must maintain those qualifications.

15—The use of all pertinent objective criteria bearing upon the personal qualifications of applicants for licenses and upon the suitability or premises proposed to be licensed is important to insure that only honest, honorable, respectable business people engage in the liquor business, and that only premises that meet standards of need, safety, decency, cleanliness, reputability, and serviceability, be covered by licenses.

Comment:

Whether these criteria are defined by statute or rule, or fixed by policy, is not vitally important, but there should be reasonable uniformity and consistency in their application.

16—Applications for licenses should be acted upon by the ABC agency as promptly as possible, with due regard both for the interests of the applicant and the public.

Comment:

It is difficult to fix arbitrarily the limits of reasonableness, since the public interest requires that applications be investigated thoroughly and since any of several valid reasons frequently prevent expeditious action on applications. Uniformity in handling all comparable applications is highly important. Where expedition and thoroughness conflict the latter consideration should prevail.

17—Persons seeking entry into the alcoholic beverage business as transferees of existing licenses, where license transfers are permitted, should meet the same standards of personal qualifications as required of applicants for original licenses, and premises to which a licensee proposes to move his business should meet the same standards for premises suitability that would be applied if an original application were being made for the premises to which removal is proposed.

Comment:

Unless these principles are adhered to, it is evident that the standards which have been fixed in the public interest will be lowered through the operation of the transfer of licenses and the removal of licensed premises. The advisability of permitting transfers of licenses is itself a debatable question. Where there has been over-licensing and the number of licenses has been limited the practice of permitting transfers has prevented reduction in the number of outlets.

18—Applicants for renewal of existing licenses should be considered in all respects in the same position as applicants for new licenses.

Comment:

This principle, of course, must be applied in the light of the fact that a good license history indicates the qualification of the applicant for renewal and of the suitability of the premises, and that conversely a record of bad, weak, or marginal operation, is good evidence of the disqualification of the applicant for renewal or the unsuitability of the premises, or both. The staggering of

61

the renewal dates of licenses according to a plan consistent with the general operations of the ABC agency should enhance the efficacy of the system requiring the annual renewal of liquor licenses.

19—Although, generally speaking, the public interest is not promoted by preventing well-qualified persons from entering the alcoholic beverage business, yet the issuance of licenses in number definitely beyond the requirements of consumers is inadvisable.

Comment:

Competition among business enterprises is the backbone of the private enterprise system and competition among licensees, as a result of which those who serve the public well succeed and those who do not do so fail, is not unwholesome. Nevertheless, there is a point beyond which ABC licenses should not be issued unless and until strong proof of need is shown. Public patronage of a specific establishment which operates in strict conformity with the requirements of law and regulation is good proof of need. A system which permits progressive licensing by issuing licenses to applicants with good qualifications and weeds out and eliminates licensees who have been found wanting in capacity, willingness and disposition to fulfill their obligations as such is the nearest approach to the ideal.

20—Faithful use of the following criteria will result in a substantial contribution to the licensing program of every ABC agency.

Comment:

These criteria require that as a prerequisite to qualification, the applicant for a license must:
(a) Be a citizen of the United States.
(b) Have a good record of law observance. If he has in the past been convicted of a crime, he must prove affirmatively that his character has been rehabilitated and that he has readjusted himself to the laws of society.
(c) Be of good repute and moral character.
(d) Have a good record of compliance if he has been previously licensed.
(e) Be at least twenty-one years of age.
(f) Be a legitimate party in the ownership interest of the business for which the license is sought. If there are other per-

sons with ownership interests in the business, such interests must be disclosed.

(g) Be independent of any interlocking industry interest which by law, regulation or policy has been denounced as inimical to good control.

(h) Be possessed of demonstrated financial responsibility to meet adequately the requirements of the business proposed to be licensed.

(i) Be independent of any official connection with any law enforcement agency having any kind or degree of responsibility for ABC enforcement, including any participation as an officer or employee of the ABC agency itself.

(j) Be able to read and write the English language and to show an understanding of the ABC law and rules.

21—Adherence to the following requirements will contribute to the success of ABC administration:

(1) The ABC agency should make available to the public informational material as to circumstances governing the issuance of licenses and the operations thereunder.

(2) All applicants should be required to make formal application in writing for a license with all statements thereunder supported by oath or affirmation, and with applicants being held strictly accountable for the accuracy, completeness and truthfulness of information thereby submitted.

(3) All such applications should be carefully examined with emphasis on the qualifications of the applicant as tested by all qualifying criteria.

(4) Close liaison should be maintained by the ABC agency with all other law enforcement agencies, and where the applicant has had any experiences in the past with any of those agencies, the full case histories should be recorded, studied and considered.

(5) Complaints of objectors who oppose the approval of the application should be given due consideration. The weight to be ascribed to such objections should be determined by the force and validity of the reasons presented in support thereof.

22—The basic provisions and procedures of control should be established by published law or rule, but the ABC agency should have broad discretionary powers to formulate administrative policy, to issue or deny licenses and penalize violators, limited only by the requirement that its action be neither arbitrary or capricious.

Comment:

It is in the interest of good control that there be available to the public definite and specific information relating to the basic requirements and prohibitions binding on applicants and licensees. To the extent that these requirements and prohibitions can be stated in definite and precise language without thereby limiting or destroying good administration or weakening control, they should in due course be incorporated either into the law or into the written rules. It is likewise in the interest of good control that those who administer it be, and be recognized as, experts in this field, and that they be held accountable as such by the public for the sound and effective administration of the law. Systems which permit outside boards of review or courts of law to substitute their judgment for that of the administrator or administrative agency do violence to this principle and make it impossible for the public to hold anyone strictly accountable for the failure to get good ABC administration, which is the usual result. Problems peculiar to the alcoholic beverage industry and to effective governmental control are numerous and involved, and they should be resolved only by experts in government with backgrounds and general qualifications known by the public to include a full understanding of and a sincere agreement with the philosophy, purposes, procedures and policies essential to effective control.

23—All agencies of government responsible in any respect for the ABC program must colloborate and coordinate their efforts, and there must be cooperation between all these agencies on the one hand and all other agencies of government on the other.

Comment:

Collaboration and cooperation of this type should never be used to confuse the respective responsibilities of the agencies involved, and there should be a clear-cut, definitive understanding by all of the respective functions of each. Shared responsibility can easily deteriorate into impaired responsibility. Cooperation by the Federal Government should include but not be limited to the following:

(a) Provide all states with the names and addresses of persons who have paid Federal occupational or manufacturing taxes;

(b) Provide for the availability as witnesses of Federal agents both in State Courts and before state ABC agencies;

(c) Referral to state ABC agencies of all information regarding violations of state ABC laws of which the Federal Government has knowledge or information.

24—The public interest requires strict compliance with rigid standards of alcoholic beverage control by a respectable and law-abiding industry, under a sound law administered by an able and upright ABC agency, supported by an informed and understanding public opinion.

TABULAR DATA

TABLE 1

STATUTORY PROVISIONS STATING THE GENERAL PURPOSES OF ALCOHOLIC BEVERAGE CONTROL

PART I—SUMMARY

State	Exercise of Police Power	Purposes Specifically Mentioned in Statutes								Other
		Welfare	Health	Peace	Morals	Protection	Safety	Promote Temperance	Prohibit Open Saloon	
Alabama	X	X	X	X	X				X	Rehabilitation and education of alcoholics.
California	X	X	X	X	X		X	X		Eliminate the evils of unlicensed and unlawful manufacture, selling and disposing of alcoholic beverages.
Colorado	X	X	X	X	X					
Georgia		X	X			X		X		Promote prosperity, growing of produce.
Idaho		X	X				X	X		
Illinois		X	X				X	X		
Indiana	X	X	X	X	X				X	
Iowa	X	X	X	X	X		X			
Louisiana	X	X	X	X	X		X			
Montana						X				
New Jersey							X	X		Eliminate racketeer and bootlegger.
New York						X	X	X	X	Promote respect for and obedience to law
Oregon	X	X	X	X	X		X	X		
Texas	X	X	X	X			X	X		
Utah	X	X	X	X	X				X	
Vermont	X	X	X	X	X		X			Exercise of taxing power; promote good order.
Washington	X	X	X	X	X		X			
West Virginia	X		X		X		X			Greatest degree of personal freedom consistent with general welfare.
Wyoming		X	X	X	X		X			
Totals	12	15	16	12	12	3	13	8	4	

69

TABLE 1

PART II—SPECIFIC PROVISIONS

ALABAMA

Title 29, Intoxicating Liquors, Chapter 1: "Sec. 2. Interpretation of chapter.—(a) This chapter shall be deemed an exercise of the police power of the State of Alabama for the protection of the public welfare, health, peace and morals of the people of the state, and to prohibit forever the open saloon; and all of the provisions of this chapter shall be liberally construed for the accomplishment of this purpose."

Governor's Act No. 115:

"AN ACT

To promote the rehabilitation of Alcoholics and to promote the education of the public with respect to Alcoholism and to make an annual appropriation for this purpose.
  Whereas, the health of its people is the primary concern of the State of Alabama, and
  Whereas, Alcoholism is recognized as a disease and the Alcoholic as a sick person, and
  Whereas, the primary task and duty of the Alcoholic Beverage Control Board is the alleviation of the ills of alcohol, and
  Whereas, the promotion of education as to alcoholism as a disease and the methods of dealing with the same is recognized as a desirable phase of education, therefore,....."

CALIFORNIA

Laws 1935, Chapter 330: "Sec. 1. This Act shall be deemed an exercise of the police powers of the State, for the protection of the safety, welfare, health, peace, and morals of the people of the State; to eliminate the evils of unlicensed and unlawful manufacture, selling and disposing of alcoholic beverages, and to promote temperance in the use and consumption of alcoholic beverages; and it is hereby declared that the subject matter of this Act involves in the highest degree the economic, social and moral well-being and the safety of the State and of all its people; and all provisions of this Act shall be liberally construed for the accomplishments of these purposes...(Sec. 1 as amended by Laws 1937, Chapter 758.)"

COLORADO

Laws 1935, Chapter 89, Article 2, Liquor Code of 1935: "Sec. 15. Exercise of police powers.—This article shall be deemed an exercise of the police powers of the state for the protection of the economic and social welfare, the health and peace and morals of the people of this state, but no provisions of this article shall ever be construed so as to authorize the establishment or maintenance of any saloon."

GEORGIA

Laws 1935, Act No. 268:

"AN ACT

To promote temperance and prosperity for Georgia people; to foster and encourage the growing of grapes, fruits and berries on Georgia farms; to legalize the making of light domestic wines; to exempt from all taxation wines made from crops of grapes, fruits and berries, whether wild or cultivated, by producers in Georgia of such crops, and to provide for the holding of an election to ratify or reject this Act, and for other purposes."

IDAHO

Laws 1947, House Bill No. 148: "Section 1. .....The restrictions, regulations, and provisions contained in this Act are enacted by the Legislature for the protection, health, welfare and safety of the people of the State of Idaho and for the purpose of promoting and encouraging temperance in the use of alcoholic beverages within said State of Idaho."

ILLINOIS

Laws 1933–1934, Second Special Session, House Bill No. 9, Article I: "Section 1. This Act shall be liberally construed, to the end that the health, safety and welfare of the People of the State of Illinois shall be protected and temperance in the consumption of alcoholic liquors shall be fostered and promoted by sound and careful control and regulation of the manufacture, sale and distribution of alcoholic liquors."

INDIANA

Laws 1935, Chapter 226: "Section 1. .....this Act shall be deemed an exercise of the police powers of the State, for the protection of the economic welfare, health, peace and morals of the people of the State, and to prohibit forever the open saloon;...."

IOWA

Code of Iowa 1946, Title VI, Chapter 123: "123.1 Public policy declared. This chapter shall be cited as the "Iowa Liquor Control Act," and shall be deemed an exercise of the state for the protection of the welfare, health, peace, morals and safety of the people of the state, and all its provisions shall be liberally construed for the accomplishment of that purpose, and it is declared to be the public policy that the traffic in alcoholic liquors is so affected with a public interest that it should be regulated to the extent of prohibiting all traffic in them, except as hereinafter provided for in this chapter through the medium of an Iowa liquor control commission by this chapter created, in which is vested the sole and exclusive authority to purchase alcoholic liquors, as defined herein, for the purpose of resale."

LOUISIANA

Laws 1948, Regular Session, Act No. 360, Title I: "WHEREAS, it is deemed necessary for the protection of the safety, welfare, health, peace and morals of the people of the State that all traffic in alcoholic beverages containing more than six per centum of alcohol by volume be regulated and controlled, and that the police power of the State be exerted so that the said traffic may not cause injury to the economic, social and moral well-being of the people of the State...."

TABLE 1—Continued

PART II—SPECIFIC PROVISIONS

MONTANA

Laws of 1937, Chapter 84: "Section 1. .....The restrictions, regulations and provisions contained in this Act are enacted by the Legislature for the protection, health, welfare and safety of the people of the State."

NEW JERSEY

Revised Statutes, 1937, Title 33, Intoxicating Liquors: "33: 1–3 It shall be the duty of the commissioner to supervise the manufacture, distribution and sale of alcoholic beverages in such a manner as to promote temperance and eliminate the racketeer and bootlegger."

NEW YORK

Laws 1934, Chapter 478, Article 1: "Sec. 2. Policy of state and purpose of chapter. It is hereby declared as the policy of the state that it is necessary to regulate and control the manufacture, sale and distribution within the state of alcoholic beverages for the purpose of fostering and promoting temperance in their consumption and respect for and obedience to law. It is hereby declared that such policy will best be carried out by empowering the liquor authority of the state to determine whether public convenience and advantage will be promoted by the issuance of licenses to traffic in alcoholic beverages, the increase or decrease in the number thereof and the location of premises licensed thereby, subject only to the right of judicial review hereinafter provided for. It is the purpose of this chapter to carry out that policy in the public interest. The restrictions regulations and provisions contained in this chapter are enacted by the legislature for the protection, health welfare and safety of the people of the state. It shall be against the public policy of the state to permit the selling or serving of alcoholic beverages for consumption in such premises as were commonly known and referred to as saloons, prior to the adoption of the eighteenth article of amendment to the constitution of the United States of America."

OREGON

Title 24, Intoxicating Liquors and Narcotics, Chapter 4, Liquor Control Act: "Sec. 24–401. Purpose of this enactment. This act shall be deemed an exercise of the police powers of the state, for the protection of the safety, welfare, health, peace and morals of the people of the state; to correct abuses existing with respect to the sale of wine; to eliminate the evils resulting from the sale within the state of wine not of proper age, soundness and general quality, and to provide for the analysis, testing and inspection of all wine before the same shall be offered for sale within the state."

Title 24, Intoxicating Liquors and Narcotics, Chapter 1: "Sec. 24–102. Purpose of act: Operation throughout state: Construction: This act shall be deemed an exercise of the police powers of the state, for the protection of the safety, welfare, health, peace and morals of the people of the state; to prevent the recurrence of abuses associated with saloons or resorts for the consumption of alcoholic beverages; to eliminate the evils of unlicensed and unlawful manufacture, selling and disposing of such beverages and to promote temperance in the use and consumption of alcoholic beverages; and it hereby is declared that the subject matter of this act involves in the highest degree the economic, social and moral well-being of the state and all of its people, and by reason thereof is a necessary subject for immediate general legislation operating uniformly throughout the state; and all provisions of this act shall be liberally construed for the accomplishment of these purposes."

TEXAS

Texas Liquor Control Act, Chapter 467, Laws 1935, Second Special Session: "Sec. 2. This entire Act shall be deemed an exercise of the police power of the State for the protection of the welfare, health, peace, temperance, and safety of the people of the State, and all of its provisions shall be liberally construed for the accomplishment of that purpose."

UTAH

Title 46, Intoxicating Liquors, Laws 1935, Chapter 43, Liquor Control Act: "46–0–44. This Act shall be deemed an exercise of the police powers of the state for the protection of the public health, peace and morals; to prevent the recurrence of abuses associated with saloons; to eliminate the evils of unlicensed and unlawful manufacture, selling and disposing of alcoholic beverages; and all provisions of this Act shall be liberally construed for the attainment of these purposes."

VERMONT

Laws 1934, Special Session, Act No. 1: "Section 1. This Act is based on the taxing power and the police power of the state, and is for the protection of the public welfare, good order, health, peace, safety and morals of the people of the state, and all of its provisions shall be liberally construed for the accomplishment of the purposes set forth herein."

WASHINGTON

Law 1933 Special Session, Chapter 62, Washington State Liquor Act: "Sec. 2. This entire Act shall be deemed an exercise of the police power of the state, for the protection of the welfare, health, peace, morals, and safety of the people of the state, and all its provisions shall be liberally construed for the accomplishment of that purpose."

WEST VIRGINIA

Code of West Virginia, 1931, Chapter 60, (As enacted by Laws 1935, Chapter 4). Article I: "Sec. 1. The purpose of this chapter is to give effect to the mandate of the people expressed in the repeal of the state prohibition amendment; and to assure the greatest degree of personal freedom that is consistent with the health, safety and good morals of the people of the state. To these ends the police power of the state is pledged to the sound control and the temperate use of alcoholic liquors."

WYOMING

Laws 1935, Chapter 87: "Section 1. For the protection of the welfare, health, peace, morals, and safety of the people of Wyoming, it is hereby declared to be a public policy in the State of Wyoming that the traffic in spirituous, fermented and malt liquors, should be regulated to the extent of prohibiting all traffic therein except as hereinafter provided, and no sale at retail of such liquors may be consummated in the State except in compliance with the provisions hereof."

71

TABLE 2

STATUTORY PROVISIONS COVERING THE COMPOSITION AND EXECUTIVE PERSONNEL OF ABC AGENCIES

State	ABC Agency Title	Number of Members of ABC Board or Commission	Administrator's Title*	Appointing Authority	Term	Salary	Bond	Qualifications			Removal
								Residence	Political	Other	
Alabama	ABC Board	3		Governor**	6 years	Expenses and $10 per diem, maximum of $1200 per annum.	Fixed by Governor.	10 years in state, qualified voter.		No interest in liquor business.	At the pleasure of the Governor.
			Administrator	ABC Board	At the pleasure of the Board.	$5,700	Fixed by Governor.	10 years in state.		No interest in liquor business; 35 years of age, good moral character.	At the pleasure of the Board.
Arizona	Department of Liquor Licenses and Control		Superintendent	Governor**	6 years	6,000	$25,000		No political activity except voting.		By the Governor for cause.
Arkansas	State Revenue Dept.		Commissioner of Revenues	Governor**	4 years			Citizen of state.		At least 30 years of age.	
California	Board of Equalization (ABC Division)	5		Elected	4 years						
			State Liquor Administrator	Board							
Colorado	Secretary of State		Secretary of State	Elected	4 years	$5,000					
Connecticut	Liquor Control Commission	3		Governor	6 years overlapping.		As regulated by Commissioner of Finance.		Not more than 2 of same party.	No interest in liquor business.	
Delaware	Liquor Commission	1		Governor	5 years		Not less than $10,000	3 years in state; qualified voter.		No interest in liquor business.	
			Executive Secretary	Commission	At the pleasure of the Commission.	Fixed by Commission.	Not less than $10,000.			No interest in liquor business.	At the pleasure of the Commission.
Florida	State Beverage Dept.		Director	Governor	4 years	$6,800	$200,000			No interest in liquor business.	At the pleasure of the Governor.

TABLE 2—Continued

STATUTORY PROVISIONS COVERING THE COMPOSITION AND EXECUTIVE PERSONNEL OF ABC AGENCIES

State	ABC Agency Title	Numbers of Members of ABC Board or Commission	Administrator's Title*	Appointing Authority	Term	Salary	Bond	Qualifications				Removal
								Residence	Political	Other		
Georgia	State Revenue Dept.		Commissioner of Revenue	Governor**	6 years							
Idaho	State Liquor Dispensary (Liquor)		Superintendent	Governor	3 years	$3,600	$25,000			No interest in liquor		At the pleasure of the Governor.
	Department of Law Enforcement (Beer)		Commissioner	Governor								
Illinois	Liquor Control Commission	3		Governor	6 years overlapping.	Chairman, $5,000. Other, $4,800.	$5,000	10 years in state.	Not more than 2 of same party.	No interest in liquor business; no conviction for felony or violation of alcoholic beverage statute.		
Indiana	Alcoholic Beverage Commission	4		Governor	4 years	$6,000 plus expenses.		10 years in state as voter or taxpayer.	Not more than 2 of same party; no political activity.	31 years old; good personal and business reputation.		
Iowa	Liquor Control Commission (Liquor)	3		Governor**	6 years overlapping.	$4,500	Fixed by Executive Council.		Not more than 2 of same party or congressional district; no political activity.			By the Governor for cause.
	State Tax Commission (Beer)	3		Governor	6 years							
Kansas	Director of Alcoholic Beverage Control (Liquor)		Director	Governor	At the pleasure of the Governor.	$7,000	Fixed by Governor. At least $50,000.					At the pleasure of the Governor.
	Board of Review (Liquor)	3		Governor	4 years overlapping.	$15 per day plus expenses.		5 years in state.		No liquor interest.		By the Governor for cause.

73

TABLE 2—Continued

STATUTORY PROVISIONS COVERING THE COMPOSITION AND EXECUTIVE PERSONNEL OF ABC AGENCIES

State	ABC Agency Title	Numbers of Members of ABC Board or Commission	Administrator's Title*	Appointing Authority	Term	Salary	Bond	Qualifications			Removal
								Residence	Political	Other	
	State Commission of Revenue and Taxation (Beer)	3		Governor**	4 years overlapping.						At the pleasure of the Governor.
Kentucky	Dept. of ABC	3	Commissioner of ABC (Chairman of ABC Board)	Governor	4 years	Chairman $5,000; Others $4,500.				Experience in ABC administration.	
Louisiana	Board of ABC	3		Governor**	6 years overlapping.	Chairman: $7,500; Others $7,000.	Fixed by Governor.			No interest in liquor business; one member from each Public Service Division.	
Maine	State Liquor Commission	3		Governor***	3 years	Expenses plus – Chairman: $6,000; Others: $4,000.			Not more than 2 of same party.	No interest in liquor business; no conviction for violation of state or federal liquor laws.	By the Governor for cause.
Maryland	Comptroller of the Treasury			Elected	4 years	$8,000.					
Massachusetts	ABC Commission	3		Governor***	3 years over-lapping.	Expenses plus – Chairman: $7,500 Others: $7,000.	Fixed by Governor.		Nor more than 2 of same party.		By the Governor. ***
Michigan	Liquor Control Commission	3		Governor**	3 years overlapping.	$7,500 plus expenses.	Fixed by Commission.		Not more than 2 of same party.		By the Governor for cause.
	Board of Hearing Examiners	3		Governor**	6 years overlapping.	$6,000 plus expenses.					

TABLE 2—Continued

STATUTORY PROVISIONS COVERING THE COMPOSITION AND EXECUTIVE PERSONNEL OF ABC AGENCIES

State	ABC Agency Title	Numbers of Members of ABC Board or Commission	Administrator's Title*	Appointing Authority	Term	Salary	Bond	Qualifications — Residence	Qualifications — Political	Qualifications — Other	Removal
Minnesota	Liquor Control Commission		Commissioner	Governor**	4 years	$4,500 plus expenses.	$50,000	Citizen and 5 years in state		No interest in liquor business.	By the Governor for cause.
Missouri	Dept. of Liquor Control		Supervisor	Governor**	At the pleasure of the Governor.	$4,500 plus expenses.	$10,000	Qualified elector; 5 years in state		Good moral character; 30 years of age.	
Montana......	Liquor Control Board	3	State Liquor Administrator	Governor** / Board	4 years overlapping. / At the pleasure of the Board.	$10 per diem, to maximum of $1,000 plus expenses. $5,400	$25,000 / Fixed by Board.	5 years in state.	Not more than 2 of same party.		By the Governor for cause. / At the pleasure of the Board.
Nebraska	Liquor Control Commission	3		Governor	6 years overlapping.	$4,000 plus expenses.	$25,000	Citizen and resident of state 2 years.	Not more than 2 of same party of same congressional district.	No interest in the liquor business; no conviction for felony.	By the Governor for cause.
Nevada	State Tax Commission	7		Governor	4 years overlapping.		$10,000				
New Hampshire	State Liquor Commission	3		Governor***	6 years	$4,000 plus expenses.	$10,000		Not more than 2 of same party.	No interest in liquor business.	By the Governor and Council for cause.
New Jersey	Division of ABC in Dept. of Law and Public Safety		Director	Governor**	During term of Governor.	$12,000	$30,000			No interest in liquor business.	
New Mexico	Bureau of Revenue (Division of Liquor Control)		Chief, Division of Liquor Control	Commissioner of Revenue	At the pleasure of Commissioner.	Set by Commissioner.				No interest in liquor business.	

TABLE 2—Continued
STATUTORY PROVISIONS COVERING THE COMPOSITION AND EXECUTIVE PERSONNEL OF ABC AGENCIES

State	ABC Agency Title	Numbers of Members of ABC Board or Commission	Administrator's Title*	Appointing Authority	Term	Salary	Bond	Qualifications			Removal
								Residence	Political	Other	
New York	State Liquor Authority	5		Governor**	5 years	Expenses plus – Chairman: $15,000; Others: $9,300.	$10,000	Citizen and resident of State	Not more than 3 of same party.	No interest in liquor business.	By the Governor for cause.
North Carolina	State Board of Alcoholic Control (Wine and Liquor) Dept. of Revenue (Beer)	3	Commissioner	Governor / Governor	3 years overlapping. / 4 years	Chairman: $6,000. Others: $7 per diem; $5,500.					By the Governor for cause.
North Dakota	State Attorney General (Liquor) State Tax Commissioner (Beer)			Elected / Elected	2 years / 4 years	$5,000.					
Ohio	Dept. of Liquor Control	4	Director-Secretary	Governor** / Governor**	4 years overlapping. / Pleasure of Governor.	$6,000, plus expenses. / $9,000, plus expenses.	$10,000 / $10,000		Not more than 2 of same party.	No interest in liquor business. / No interest in liquor business.	By the Governor for cause. / By the Governor for cause.
Oregon	Liquor Control Commission	3	Administrator	Governor / Commission	6 years overlapping. / At the pleasure of the commission.	Expenses, plus $10 per diem.	$5,000 / $25,000	5 years in state.	not more than 2 of same party or of same congressional district.	At least 30 years of age; no interest in liquor business.	By the Governor for cause.
Pennsylvania	Liquor Control Board	3		Governor**	6 years overlapping.	$10,000	$10,000	Resident and elector of state 1 year.		At least 30 years of age; no other public office; no interest in liquor business.	

76

TABLE 2—Continued

STATUTORY PROVISIONS COVERING THE COMPOSITION AND EXECUTIVE PERSONNEL OF ABC AGENCIES

State	ABC Agency Title	Numbers of Members of ABC Board or Commission	Administrator's Title*	Appointing Authority	Term	Salary	Bond	Qualifications Residence	Qualifications Political	Qualifications Other	Removal
Rhode Island	Dept. of Business Regulation		Liquor Control Administrator	Division of Dept. of Business Regulation with approval of Governor.							
	Liquor Control Hearing Board	3		Governor	6 years overlapping.	$25 per day up to $1,000 per year.			Not more than 2 of same party.		By Governor for cause.
South Carolina	State Tax Commission	3		Governor**	6 years overlapping.						By the Governor.**
South Dakota	Dept. of Finance Div. of Licensing		Director	Governor	At the pleasure of the Governor.					No interest in liquor business.	At the pleasure of the Governor.
Tennessee	Dept. of Finance and Taxation		Commissioner	Governor	2 years	$6,600					
Texas	Liquor Control Board	3	Administrator	Governor** / Board	6 years overlapping. / At the pleasure of the Board.	Expenses plus $10 per diem; maximum 60 days. / $6,000	$10,000	5 years in state; qualified voter.		No interest in liquor business. / No interest in liquor business.	At the pleasure of the Board.
Utah	Liquor Control Commission	3		Governor	6 years overlapping.	$4,000	Fixed by Dept. of Finance.		Not more than 2 of same party.		At the pleasure of the Governor.
Vermont	Liquor Control Board	3	Liquor Administrator	Governor** / Board with approval of Governor.	6 years overlapping. Pleasure of Board.	Expenses plus $10 per diem. / $3,250–$4,500.			Not more than 2 of same party.		By the Governor for cause. / At the pleasure of the Board.

77

TABLE 2—Continued

STATUTORY PROVISIONS COVERING THE COMPOSITION AND EXECUTIVE PERSONNEL OF ABC AGENCIES

State	ABC Agency Title	Numbers of Members of ABC Board or Commission	Administrator's Title*	Appointing Authority	Term	Salary	Bond	Qualifications			Removal
								Residence	Political	Other	
Virginia.......	ABC Board	3		Governor	5 years overlapping.	$7,500	Fixed by Governor.			No interest in liquor business.	At the pleasure of the Governor.
Washington....	Liquor Control Board	3		Governor**	6 years overlapping.	$7,500	$50,000			No other public office.	At the pleasure of the Governor.
West Virginia	Liquor Control Commission (Liquor)	3		Governor**	4 years overlapping.	Expenses plus $6,000.	$25,000		Not more than 2 of same party.	"Ability and fitness"; no interest in liquor business; no other public office. At least 30 years of age.	
	Non-intoxicating Beer Commissioner (Beer)		Commissioner	Governor**	6 years	$6,000	Fixed by Governor.	Resident for 1 year.			
Wisconsin	State Treasurer			Elected	2 years	$6,500					
Wyoming	Liquor Commission	5	Director	Ex officio elected state officials. Liquor Commission	At the pleasure of the Commission.	$5,600					At the pleasure of the Commission.
District of Columbia	ABC Board	3		District of Columbia Commissioners.	4 years overlapping.	In accordance with Classification Act.		Citizen: 3 consecutive, immediately preceding years in the District.		No interest in liquor business.	At the pleasure of the Commissioners.

* This schedule contains only such data on administrative officials as is set forth explicitly by statute.
** With advice and consent of the Senate.
*** With advice and consent of the Council.

TABLE 3

STATE AGENCIES ADMINISTERING ALCOHOLIC BEVERAGE TAXES
(As Reported in Questionnaire Replies)

State	Principal ABC Agency	Agency with Principal Responsibility for Administering Alcoholic Beverage Taxes (if Different from ABC Agency)
Alabama	ABC Board	—
Arkansas	State Revenue Dept.	—
California	Board of Equalization	—
Colorado	Secretary of State	Dept. of Revenue
Connecticut	Liquor Control Commission	State Tax Department
Delaware	Liquor Commission	—
Florida	State Beverage Dept.	—
Georgia	State Revenue Dept.	—
Idaho	State Liquor Dispensary (Liquor)	—
	Dept. of Law Enforcement (Beer)	—
Illinois	Liquor Control Commission	Dept. of Revenue
Indiana	Alcoholic Beverage Commission	—
Iowa	Liquor Control Commission (Liquor)	—
	State Tax Commission (Beer)	
Kentucky	Dept. of Alcoholic Beverage Control	Dept. of Revenue
Maryland	Alcoholic Beverage Division	Comptroller of the Treasury
Michigan	Liquor Control Commission	—
Minnesota	Liquor Control Commission	State Treasurer
Missouri	Dept. of Liquor Control	—
Nebraska	Liquor Control Commission	—
Nevada	State Tax Commission	—
New Hampshire	State Liquor Commission	—
New Jersey	Dept. of Law and Public Safety—Division of Alcoholic Beverage Control	Dept. of the Treasury
New Mexico	Bureau of Revenue—Division of Liquor Control	
New York	State Liquor Authority	Dept. of Taxation and Finance
North Carolina	State Board of Alcoholic Control	Dept. of Revenue
North Dakota	Attorney General (Liquor)	State Treasurer
	State Tax Commission (Beer)	—
Ohio	Dept. of Liquor Control	State Tax Commission
Oregon	Liquor Control Commission	—
Pennsylvania	Liquor Control Board	Dept. of Revenue
Rhode Island	Dept. of Business Regulation	Division of Taxation
South Carolina	State Tax Commission	—
South Dakota	Dept. of Finance—Division of Licensing	—
Vermont	Liquor Control Board	Commissioner of Taxes
Virginia	Alcoholic Beverage Control Board	Commissioner of Taxation
Washington	Liquor Control Board	—
West Virginia	Liquor Control Commission (Liquor)	—
	Non-intoxicating Beer Commissioner (Beer)	—
Wisconsin	State Treasurer	—
District of Columbia	Alcoholic Beverage Control Board	Collector of Taxes

79

TABLE 4

TERMS OF GOVERNORS, AND NUMBER AND TERMS OF ABC PERSONNEL SUBJECT TO APPOINTMENT BY GOVERNOR

State	Term of Governor (years)	Special Conditions Applicable to Term of Governor	Board or Commission[a] Number	Board or Commission[a] Term (years)	Administrator[a] Term (years)
Alabama	4	Cannot succeed himself	3	6	—
Arizona	2	—	—	—	6
Arkansas	2	—	—	—	4
California	4	—	—	—	—
Colorado	2	—	—	—	—
Connecticut	2	—	3	6 (overlapping)	—
Delaware	4	Cannot succeed himself after 2 consecutive terms	1	5	—
Florida	4	Cannot succeed himself	—	—	4
Georgia	4	—	—	—	6
Idaho	4	Cannot succeed himself	Liquor — Beer —	— —	3 —
Illinois	4	—	3	6 (overlapping)	—
Indiana	4	Cannot succeed himself	4[b]	4	—
Iowa	2	—	Liquor 3 Beer 3	6 (overlapping) 6	— —
Kansas	2	May not be elected to more than 2 terms	Liquor 3 Beer 3	— 4 (overlapping)	Pleasure of Governor —
Kentucky	4	Cannot succeed himself	3	4	e
Louisiana	4	Cannot succeed himself	3	6 (overlapping)	—
Maine	2	—	3	3 e	—
Maryland	4	—	—	—	e1
Massachusetts	2	—	3	3 e(overlapping)	—
Michigan	2	—	3	3 (overlapping) 6 (overlapping)	—
Minnesota	2	—	—	—	4
Missouri	4	Cannot succeed himself	—	—	Pleasure of Governor
Montana	4	—	3	4 (overlapping)	—
Nebraska	2	—	3	6 (overlapping)	—
Nevada	4	—	7[d]	4 (overlapping)	—
New Hampshire	2	—	3	6 e	—
New Jersey	3	—	—	—	—
New Mexico	2	Cannot succeed himself after 2 consecutive terms for 2 terms thereafter	—	—	—
New York	4	—	5	5	—
North Carolina	4	Cannot succeed himself	Wine and Liquor 3 Beer —	3 (overlapping) —	— 4
North Dakota	2	—	—	—	—
Ohio	2	—	4	4 (overlapping)	Pleasure of Governor
Oregon	4	May not be elected to more than 2 terms	3	6 (overlapping)	—
Pennsylvania	4	Cannot succeed himeslf	3	6 (overlapping)	—
Rhode Island	2	—	3	6 (overlapping)	e
South Carolina	4	Cannot succeed himself	3	6 (overlapping)	—
South Dakota	2	Cannot succeed himself after 2 consecutive terms	—	—	Pleasure of Governor
Tennessee	2	Shall not be eligible for office more than 6 years in any period of 8 years	—	—	2
Texas	2	—	3	6 (overlapping)	—
Utah	4	—	3	6 (overlapping)	—
Vermont	2	—	3	6 (overlapping)	e
Virginia	4	—	3	5 (overlapping)	—
Washington	4	—	3	6 (overlapping)	—
West Virginia	4	Cannot succeed himself	Liquor 3 Beer —	4 (overlapping) —	— 6
Wisconsin	2	—	—	—	—
Wyoming	4	—	f	—	—
Dist. of Columbia	—	—	—	—	—

[a] Appointment usually subject to advice and consent of Senate, or, in the case of Maine, New Hampshire, and Massachusetts, of the Governor's Council.

[b] In the event that the Governor and Lieutenant Governor are not members of the same political party, the latter's consent must be obtained for the appointment of two of the members.

[e] Chairman of the ABC Board is also the Commissioner of Alcoholic Beverage control and as such is responsible for the administration of the ABC Act.

[e1] Appointed by Comptroller of the Treasury who is elected for four years.

[d] Governor is one of the seven commission members.

[e] Governor must approve appointment of Administrator by ABC agency.

[f] Governor is one member of five-man ex-officio commission.

TABLE 5

STATUTORY PROVISIONS COVERING THE RULE-MAKING POWER OF STATE ABC AGENCIES

ALABAMA

Code of Alabama, 1940. Title 29—Intoxicating Liquors, Chapter 1:

"Sec. 6. The board may from time to time make such regulations not inconsistent with this chapter as it shall deem necessary for carrying out the provisions of this chapter, and from time to time alter, repeal, or amend such regulations, or any of them."

ARIZONA

Arizona Code 1939. Chapter 72—Spirituous Liquors, Article 1:

"72–103. (b) The superintendent shall have power: 1. to prescribe necessary rules and regulations: 1a. for carrying out the provisions of this Act; 1b. for the proper conduct of the business to be carried on under each specific type of spirituous liquor license; 1c. to enable and assist state officials to collect all taxes levied or imposed in connection with spirituous liquors; and, 1d. to procure full compliance by licensees, in the conduct of their business, with all laws."

ARKANSAS

Acts 1935, Act 69—Wine Law:

"Sec. 11.....the Commissioner shall from time to time promulgate reasonable rules and regulations or the effective enforcement and administration of this Act, and the collection of the taxes, fees, and licenses herein provided....." Acts 1935. Act 108—The Arkansas Alcoholic Control Act:

"Sec. 3. The Commissioner of Revenues shall have the following powers, functions and duties:....(c) To adopt rules and regulations for the supervision and control of the manufacture and sale of vinous (except wines), spirituous or malt liquors throughout the State not inconsistent with law."

CALIFORNIA

Laws 1935. Chapter 330:

"Sec. 38. The board shall make and prescribe such reasonable rules and regulations as may be necessary or proper to carry out the purposes and intent of Section 22 of Article XX of the Constitution and to enable it to exercise the powers and perform the duties conferred upon it by said section or by the provisions of this act, not inconsistent with any of the provisions of any statute of this State....."

COLORADO

Laws 1935. Chapter 89, Article 2:

"Sec. 20. .....The Secretary of state shall be the executive in charge of the enforcement of the terms and provisions of this article, and as the state licensing authority his duties and authority shall be as follows:... (b) To make such general rules and regulations and such special rulings and findings as he may deem necessary for the proper regulation and control of the manufacture, sale and distribution of malt, vinous or spirituous liquors and the enforcement of this article, in addition thereto, and not inconsistent therewith, and may alter, amend, repeal and publish the same from time to time."

CONNECTICUT

General Statutes of Connecticut, Chapter 151—Liquor Control Act, Article II:

"Sec. 619h......The commission shall have power to enforce the provisions of this chapter, and to make all needful rules and regulations for that purpose and for carrying out, enforcing and preventing violation of, all or any of the provisions of this chapter, for the inspection of permit premises and the method of carrying on the business of any permittee, for insuring sanitary conditions, for insuring proper, safe and orderly conduct of licensed premises and for protecting the public against fraud or overcharge...."

DELAWARE

Revised Code of Delaware, 1935. Chapter 176—Alcoholic Liquor, Wines and Beer:

"6134. Sec. 5. The functions, duties and powers of the Commission shall be the following: (1) To adopt and promulgate rules and regulations not inconsistent with the provisions of this Chapter or of the laws of the State of Delaware. All such rules and regulations shall have the force and effect of law....." Authorizations to promulgate certain rules and regulations are made throughout the statute.

FLORIDA

Florida Statutes 1941, Title XXXII, Chapter 561:

"561.08 .....the director shall prescribe forms of bonds, reports and other papers, and rules and regulations not inconsistent with law, to be used under and in the execution and enforcement of the provisions of the beverage law."

GEORGIA

Laws 1937–38, Special Session. Act No. 297:

"Sec. 8. The State Revenue Commissioner shall have the following powers and duties:....(f) To issue rules and regulations governing all advertising of distilled spirits within this state. (g) To issue rules and regulations not inconsistent with the Federal laws or regulations requiring informative labeling of all distilled spirits offered for sale hereunder. (h) To adopt and promulgate, repeal and amend such rules, regulations, standards, requirements and orders not inconsistent with this Act or any law of this state or of the United States as he may deem necessary to control the manufacture, sale, distribution, storage, or transportation of distilled spirits and alcohol in accordance with the provisions of this Act, and the conditions under which same may be withdrawn from said warehouses and distributed."

IDAHO

Laws 1939. Chapter 222—Idaho Liquor Act, Article I:

"Sec. 307 (b) To promulgate rules and regulations in the exercise of the governmental and proprietary powers and duties of the dispensary."

TABLE 5—Continued

STATUTORY PROVISIONS COVERING THE RULE-MAKING POWER
OF STATE ABC AGENCIES

ILLINOIS

Laws 1933–34, Second Special Session. House Bill No. 9—Liquor Control Act, Article I:

"Sec. 12. The Commission shall have the following powers, functions, and duties: (4) To recommend to local commissioners rules and regulations, not inconsistent with law, for the distribution and sale of alcoholic liquors throughout the State." The Commission also has authority to adopt rules governing the manufacture and labeling of alcoholic beverages.

INDIANA

Laws 1935. Chapter 226—Alcoholic Beverages Act of 1935:

Throughout the statute there are authorizations to promulgate certain rules and regulations. In addition, n Section 6 the following is stated: "The foregoing enumeration of powers of said commission or of said excise administrator shall not impair or prejudice any other power herein expressly or impliedly granted to said commission or said administrator by any other provision of this Act."

IOWA

Code of Iowa, 1946. Title VI—Alcoholic Beverages, Chapter 123:

"123.17. 1. The commission may make such rules and regulations not inconsistent with this chapter, which to the commission may seem expedient or necessary for carrying out the provisions of this chapter and for the efficient administration thereof."

KANSAS

Laws 1935. Chapter 79, Article 38 (Cereal Malt Beverages):

"Sec. 79–3835.....The director with the approval of the commission, shall prescribe such reasonable rules and regulations as may be necessary for the efficient administration of this Act."

Laws 1949. Senate Bill No. 9—Kansas Liquor Control Act:

"Sec.15.....The director shall adopt and promulgate such rules and regulations as shall be necessary to carry out the intent and purposes of this act. All rules and regulations of general application, including the amendment or repeal thereof to implement or make specific this act, shall first be submitted by the director to the Board [of Review] for its approval, and upon approval shall be filed in the office of the revisor of statutes as provided by article 4 of chapter 77 of the General Statutes Supplement of 1947....."

KENTUCKY

Title XX. Chapter 241—Alcoholic Beverages—Administration and Control:

"241.060. Functions of board. The board shall have the following functions, powers and duties: (1) To adopt reasonable regulations governing the procedure relative to applications for and revocations of licenses and relative to all other matters over which the board has jurisdiction, and for the supervision and control of the manufacture, sale, transportation, storage, advertising and trafficking of alcoholic beverages. Regulations need not be uniform in their application, but may vary in accordance with reasonable classifications..... (8) To make rules and regulations, and to provide forms, that may be necessary to regulate the alcoholic beverage industry....."

LOUISIANA

Law 1948, Regular Session. Act No. 360—Alcoholic Beverage Control Act, Title I:

"Sec. 11.....It (the Louisiana Board of Alcoholic Beverage Control) shall also have power to adopt from time to time,.....reasonable rules, regulations and modes of procedure, which have the effect of law, for the administration of this Act, not inconsistent with this Act or other law of the state or of the United States...... "

MAINE

Revised Statutes of Maine, 1944. Title 8—Chapter 57:

"VIII. To establish regulations for clarifying, carrying out, enforcing, and preventing violation of all or any of the laws pertaining to liquor, which regulations shall have the force and effect of law unless and until set aside by some court or competent jurisdiction or revoked by the commission."

MARYLAND

Annoted Code of Maryland. Article 2B—Alcoholic Beverages:

"Sec. 157......In addition to the powers otherwise provided by this Article, the Comptroller, the Board of License Commissioners from any County or Baltimore City, or the State Appeal Board shall, respectively, have full power and authority to adopt such reasonable rules and regulations as they may deem necessary to enable them effectively to discharge the duties imposed upon them by this Article."

MASSACHUSETTS

Tercentary Edition 1932 (As Amended). Chapter 138—Alcoholic Liquors:

"Sec. 24. The commission shall, with the approval of the governor and council, make regulations not inconsistent with the provisions of this chapter for clarifying, carrying out, enforcing and preventing violation of all and any of its provisions....."

MICHIGAN

Laws, First Special Session 1933. Public Act No. 8—Liquor Control Act:

"Sec. 7. The commission shall adopt rules and regulations governing the carrying out of this act and the duties and responsibilities of licensees in the proper conduct and management of their licensed places."

TABLE 5—Continued

STATUTORY PROVISIONS COVERING THE RULE-MAKING POWER
OF STATE ABC AGENCIES

MINNESOTA

Statutes 1945. Chapter 340—Intoxicating Liquors:

"340.09.....The commissioner shall have power to make all reasonable regulations to effect the object of sections 340.07 to 340.96......"

(Sections 340.07 to 340.96 comprise the entire chapter with the exception of sections 340.01 to 340.06 which are concerned with beer. Regulatory power over beer is given to local governing bodies.

MISSISSIPPI

Code of 1942 (As Amended). Title 40, Chapter 5, Division 3:

"Sec. 10242.....and the method of affixing such stamps and method of cancellation shall be prescribed by the Commissioner, who is hereby authorized to promulgate rules and regulations covering the method of affixing and cancelling of such stamps."

"Sec. 10253.....It shall be the duty of the Commissioner to prescribe and promulgate uniform rules and regulations for keeping such records and making such reports."

MISSOURI

Revised Statutes 1939. Chapter 32—Intoxicating and Nonintoxicating Liquors, Article 1:

Section 4889 states: ".....the Supervisor of Liquor Control shall have the authority to.....make the following regulations (without limiting the generality of provisions empowering the Supervisor of Liquor Control as in this Act set forth) as to the following matters, acts and things;....." After a detailed discussion of such "matters, acts and things," the section closes with this terminology: ".....and to make such other rules and regulations as are necessary and feasible for carrying out the provisions of this Act, as are not inconsistent with this Act."

MONTANA

Laws 1937. Chapter 84—Retail Sales Law:

(Retail Sales Law) "Sec. 22. For the purpose of the administration of this Act, the Board shall make, promulgate and publish such rules and regulations as the said Board may deem necessary for carrying out the provisions of this Act and for the orderly and efficient administration hereof, and except as may be limited or prohibited by law and the provisions of this Act, such rules and regulations so made and promulgated shall have the force of statute."

Revised Codes of 1935. Political Code, Chapter 254—Montana Beer Act:

"Sec. 2815.12. (b) Without in any way limiting or being limited by the foregoing, the board may make such regulations as are necessary and feasible for the purpose of carrying into effect the provisions of this act, and such regulations shall have the full force and effect of law."

Laws 1935. Chapter 255—State Liquor Control:

"Sec. 2815.68. (1) The board may make such regulations, not inconsistent with this act, as to the board seem necessary, for carrying out the provisions of this act, and for the efficient administration thereof."

NEBRASKA

Revised Statutes of 1942. Chapter 53—Liquors:

"53–117. Commission; powers and duties.....it is intended by this grant of the power to adopt rules and regulations, that the commission shall be clothed with broad discretionary powers to govern the traffic in alcoholic liquors, and to enforce strictly all the provisions of this act in the interest of sanitation, purity of products, truthful representations and honest dealings in such manner as generally will promote the public health and welfare....."

NEVADA

Laws 1935. Chapter 160—Nevada Liquor Law:

"Sec. 22. The commission is hereby charged and empowered with the duty of administrating the provisions of this act, and it shall adopt and enforce all rules, regulations and standards necessary to carry out the provisions of this act."

NEW HAMPSHIRE

Title XVI—Regulations of Police. Chapter 170—Spirituous Liquors and Beverages:

"Sec. 12. Rules and Regulations.—Said commission shall have power to make all necessary and proper rules and regulations for carrying out the provisions hereof, and such rules and regulations shall have the effect of law."

"Sec. 81. Rules.—The commission may from time to time prescribe such rules and regulations not inconsistent with law as it may deem necessary for the issuance of permits and for the possession, manufacture, transportation, sale, offer for sale, or solicitation of orders for sale of beverages, the operation of the business of permittees, and for any other purpose required for the efficient execution of this subdivision."

NEW JERSEY

Revised Statutes, 1937. Title 33—Intoxicating Liquors:

"33:1-39. Rules and regulations by commissioner; subjects covered. The commissioner may make such general rules and regulations and such special rulings and findings as may be necessary for the proper regulation and control of the manufacture, sale and distribution of alcoholic beverages and the enforcement of this chapter, in addition thereto, and not inconsistent therewith, and may alter, amend, repeal and publish the same from time to time."

TABLE 5—Continued

STATUTORY PROVISIONS COVERING THE RULE-MAKING POWER
OF STATE ABC AGENCIES

NEW JERSEY—(Cont.)

This section goes on to specify which subjects may be covered by such rules and regulations, ending with the following statement: "....and such other matters whatsoever as are or may become necessary in the fair, impartial, stringent, and comprehensive administration of this chapter."

"33: 1–39. 1. Reciprocal rules and regulations with other states. The commissioner may make such reciprocal rules and regulations and special rulings pertaining to any one or more states designated therein as may be necessary for the proper regulation and control of the manufacture, sale and distribution of alcoholic beverages and the enforcement of this chapter, in addition thereto and not inconsistent therewith, and alter, amend, repeal and publish the same from time to time."

"33: 1–93. (Regulation by state commissioner.) The State Commissioner of Alcoholic Beverage Control is hereby vested with power to promulgate such rules and regulations on the following subjects as will assist in properly supervising the liquor industry and promoting temperance: (a) maximum discounts, rebates, free goods, allowances and other inducements to retailers by manufacturers, wholesalers and other persons privileged to sell to retailers; (b) gifts and deliveries of money, products and other things of value by manufacturers, wholesalers, other persons privileged to sell to retailers, their stockholders, officers, directors and employees; (c) maintenance and publication of invoice prices, discounts, rebates, free goods, allowances and other inducements; and (d) such other matters as may be necessary to fulfill the restrictions embodied in this act."

NEW MEXICO

Statutes 1941. Chapter 61—Intoxicating Liquors, Article 1:

"61–204. It shall be the duty of the chief of division: (a) To......distribute......among the licensees and persons to be affected or governed thereby copies of all rules and regulations established and promulgated under the provisions of this act......"

Article 6:

"61–601. Whenever the chief of division in any hearing in this article provided for, which hearing is conducted in substantial compliance with the provisions of this article, shall find that any liquor licensee has:.... (c) refused to comply with any valid rule or regulation adopted and promulgated under the provisions of this act by the chief of division or commissioner;......he may suspend or revoke the license of such licensee."

Other than the above no specific mention is made of regulatory power.

NEW YORK

Laws 1934. Chapter 478 (Chapter 3–B of the Consolidated Laws Alcoholic Beverage Control Law), Article 1:

"Sec. 115. Rules need not be uniform. Whenever in this chapter the liquor authority is authorized to adopt rules in respect to a particular subject or matter, such rules need not be uniform in their application to the various localities within the jurisdiction of such authority, but may vary in accordance with a reasonable classification of such localities."

"Sec. 17. Powers of the authority.....5. To fix by rule the standards of manufacture and fermentation in order to insure the use of proper ingredients and methods in the manufacture of alcoholic beverages to be sold or consumed in the state."

"Sec. 101-C. To promulgate rules to carry out the purpose of this section requiring brand owners of liquor and wine to file schedules of minimum consumer resale prices which are controlling upon all licensed retailers of those brands."

NORTH CAROLINA

General Statutes, 1943. Chapter 18—Regulation of Intoxicating Liquors, Article 3:

"Sec. 18–39. (m) The said state board shall have all other powers which may be reasonably implied from the granting of express powers herein named, together with such other powers as may be incidental to, or convenient for, the carrying out and performance of the powers and duties herein given to said board."

NORTH DAKOTA

No statutory provisions.

OHIO

Liquor Control Act, Section 6064–3:

"The board of liquor control shall have power except as otherwise provided in this section:
1. To adopt and promulgate, repeal, rescind, and amend, in the manner herein required, rules, regulations, standards, requirements, and orders necessary to carry out the provisions of the liquor control act and amendments thereof, including the following:" (lists a considerable number in detail).

OKLAHOMA

No statutory provisions.

OREGON

Title 24—Intoxicating Liquors and Narcotics. Chapter 1—Liquor Control Act:

"Sec. 24–106. (h) To adopt such regulations as are necessary and feasible for carrying out the provisions of this Act, and to amend or repeal such regulations. When such regulations are adopted as herein provided they shall have the full force and effect of law. Any person violating such regulation shall, upon conviction thereof, be punished by a fine of not more than two hundred dollars ($200), or by imprisonment in the county jail for not more than three (3) months, or by both such fine and imprisonment, in the discretion of the court."

PENNSYLVANIA

Alcohol License Law, 1926 (As Amended):

"Sec. 17. The board shall have the power to make and promulgate appropriate rules and regulations for carrying into effect the provisions of this act. (Amended by Act No. 9 of December 8, 1933, P. L. 57; as reenacted in Act. No. 371 of June 16, 1937, P. L. 1811.)"

TABLE 5—Continued

STATUTORY PROVISIONS COVERING THE RULE-MAKING POWER
OF STATE ABC AGENCIES

RHODE ISLAND

Laws of 1938. Title XX—Alcoholic Beverage, Chapter 162:

"Sec. 5. .....and said department is hereby authorized to establish rules and regulations and to authorize the making of such rules and regulations by the licensing authority of the several towns and cities as in their respective discretions in the public interest shall seem proper to be made."

SOUTH CAROLINA

Code of Laws of South Carolina 1942, Chapter 107:

"Sec. 2557–3.....The South Carolina tax commission is hereby authorized, empowered, and directed to promulgate rules and regulations for the payment and collection of taxes hereby levied."
"Sec. 2557–12. .....(3) .....The South Carolina tax commission shall have authority and it is hereby required to make such rules and regulations for the operation of breweries and commercial wineries authorized hereunder."

"2557–16. ......and said commission is also empowered to make regulations as to containers in which wine may be sold at retail and to declare to be 'undesirable wine packages' any wine sold in a container prohibited in such regulations......"

SOUTH DAKOTA

South Dakota Code of 1939. Title 5—Alcoholic Beverages Chapter 5.01:

"5.0102......He (the director of the Division of Licensing) shall promulgate rules and regulations as provided by this Code as to rules and regulations of state boards and officials, and which must include suitable rules for conducting all hearings provided for by this title, the giving of notice thereof, and preservation of an adequate record, and may include any reasonable regulations not inconsistent with this title or with federal laws or regulations, to effect the objects of this title, including, among others, regulations to insure purity of alcoholic beverages and true statements as to the contents of any container thereof and may, if the (director of the Division of Licensing) deems it advisable, prohibit or regulate advertising of intoxicating liquor."

TENNESSEE

Public Acts 1939. Chapter 49:

"Sec. 4 (3) The Commissioner shall have and exercise the following functions, duties and powers, to wit: (b) To make, promulgate, alter, amend or repeal rules and regulations for the enforcement of this Act or the collection of all license fees and taxes, and all penalties and forfeitures relating thereto."

Public Acts 1933. Chapter 69:

"Sec. 8. ......The commissioner of finance and taxation is hereby authorized and it shall be his duty to make rules and regulations necessary in his opinion to carry out the provisions of this act, which rules and regulations shall have the force and effect of law if not in conflict with express statutory provisions."

TEXAS

Laws 1935, Second Special Session. Chapter 407—Texas Liquor Control Act, Article I:

"Sec. 6. Among others, the functions, powers, and duties of the Board shall include the following: (a) To supervise, inspect, and regulate every phase of the business of manufacturing, importation, transportation, storage, sale, distribution, possession for the purpose of sale, and possession of all alcoholic beverages, including the advertising and labeling thereof, in all respects necessary to accomplish the purposes of this act. The Board is hereby vested with power and authority to prescribe all necessary rules and regulations to that end;.....to supervise and regulate all licensees and permittees and their places of business in all matters affecting the general public, whether herein specifically mentioned or not......"
"Sec. 7 (a). No rule or regulation for which a penalty is prescribed either by this Act or by the Board, shall be adopted by the Board except after notice and hearing."

UTAH

Title 46—Intoxicating Liquors, Laws 1935. Chapter 43—Liquor Control Act:

"46–0–49. The commission may, from time to time, make such resolutions, orders and regulations, not inconsistent with this Act, as it may deem necessary for carrying out the provisions thereof and for its efficient administration. The commission shall cause such regulations to be filed in the office of the secretary of state, and thereupon they shall have the same force as if they formed a part of this Act. The commission may amend or repeal such regulations, and such amendments or repeals shall be filed in the same manner, and with like effect. The commission may from time to time cause such regulations to be printed for distribution in such manner as it may deem proper."

VERMONT

Laws 1934, Special Session. Act No. 1—Liquor Control Act:

"Sec 12. V. Make and promulgate regulations necessary for the execution of its powers and duties and ot the powers and duties of all persons under its supervision and control."

VIRGINIA

Laws 1933, First Special Session, Chapter 3—Beer and Light Wine Law:

"Sec. 5. The board shall likewise have the same power to pass regulations having the force and effect of law necessary to carry out the provisions and purposes of this Act, and to prevent the illegal manufacture, bottling, sale, distribution and transportation of beverages, or any one or more of such illegal acts, and from time to time alter, repeal or amend such regulations, or any of them. Such regulations shall be published in the same manner as regulations are required to be published under the Alcoholic Beverage Control Act."

TABLE 5—Continued

STATUTORY PROVISIONS COVERING THE RULE-MAKING POWER OF STATE ABC AGENCIES

VIRGINIA—Continued

Laws 1934—Chapter 94—Alcoholic Beverage Control Act:

"Sec. 5. Power to make regulations; how published; effect thereof. (a) The board may from time to time make such reasonable regulations, not inconsistent with this Act, nor the general laws of the State, as the board shall deem necessary to carry out the purposes and provisions of this Act and to prevent the illegal manufacture, bottling, sale, distribution and transportation of alcoholic beverages, or any one or more of such illegal acts, and from time to time alter, repeal, or amend such regulations or any of them. Such regulations shall be published at least once in some newspaper published in the city of Richmond and in any other manner which the board may deem advisable, and upon being so published shall have the force and effect of law. The board shall certify to the clerks of all circuit courts and city courts of record having criminal jurisdiction copies of all regulations adopted by the board; such clerks shall keep on file for public inspection all such regulations certified to them by the board. (b) Nothing in this Act contained shall require such regulations to be uniform in their application. (c) Justices and courts shall take judicial notice of the regulations of the board made, published and filed in accordance with the provisions of this Act."

WASHINGTON

Laws 1933, Special Session. Chapter 62—Washington State Liquor Act:

"Sec 79. (1) For the purpose of carrying into effect the provisions of this Act according to their true intent or of supplying any deficiency therein, the board may make such regulations not inconsistent with the spirit of this Act as are deemed necessary or advisable. All regulations so made shall be a public record and filed in the office of the Secretary of State, together with a copy of this Act, shall forthwith be published in pamphlets, which pamphlets shall be distributed free at all liquor stores and as otherwise directed by the board, and thereupon shall have the same force and effect as if incorporated in this Act."

WEST VIRGINIA

Laws 1935. Chapter 4—Liquor Control Act:

"Art. II. Sec. 11. (1) Liquor commission may exercise general supervision of and make rules and regulations for the management of its department. Sec. 15. The commission shall prescribe regulations governing the advertising of alcoholic liquors in this state. The regulations shall prohibit advertising that encourages intemperance, induces minors to purchase, or tends to deceive or misrepresent."

"Art. IV. Sec. 17. The commission shall have the authority to prescribe such rules and regulations and to require the reporting of such information by licensees as may be necessary for the effective administration of the provisions of this chapter."

WISCONSIN

Chapter 139—Emergency Occupational Tax on Malt Beverages:
"Sec. 139.03 (11). The state treasurer.....shall issue such rules and regulations as may be necessary to carry out the provisions of this chapter."

Chapter 176—Intoxicating Liquors:

"Sec. 176.43 (2) The state treasurer in furtherance of effective control may promulgate rules and regulations consistent with chapter 66 (General Municipality Law) and chapter 139 (Emergency Occupational Tax on Malt Beverages)."

In addition, authority to prescribe regulations on specific subjects is granted by various provisions throughout the statutes.

WYOMING

Laws 1935. Chapter 117—Wyoming Liquor Commission:

"Sec. 2. (e) The Wyoming Liquor Commission is hereby given the right and authority, and is hereby directed to make such rules and regulations as it may deem necessary to carry out the provisions of this Act."

DISTRICT OF COLUMBIA

Act of 1935. Section 7. "The Commissioners are hereby authorized to prescribe such rules and regulations not inconsistent with this Act as they may deem necessary to carry out the purposes thereof and to control and regulate the manufacture, sale, keeping for sale, offer for sale, solicitation of orders for sale, importation, exportation and transportation of alcoholic beverages in the District of Columbia for the protection of the public health, comfort, safety, and morals."

TABLE 6

METHODS USED TO NOTIFY INTERESTED PARTIES AND THE PUBLIC OF NEW OR CHANGED RULES AND REGULATIONS

(As Reported by Questionnaire Replies)

State	Method
Alabama	Copies furnished to interested parties.
Arkansas	New rules filed in office of Secretary of State. Newspapers are notified.
California	Filed with Secretary of State and published in Administrative Code and Administrative Register.
Colorado	Notice mailed to all Colorado licensees. Copies mailed to Commerce Clearing House.
Connecticut	Must be published in at least one newspaper in each county, and also in Connecticut Law Journal.
Delaware	Rules and regulations disseminated by conference and mail.
Florida	Regulations pertaining to wholesalers are mailed to each wholesaler. Press releases inform retailers.
Georgia	None.
Idaho	Interested parties notified by bulletin.
Illinois	Notification of regulations by publication in trade press and by distribution of copies among members of the industry.
Indiana	Published twice in newspaper of general circulation.
Iowa	None.
Kentucky	Copies of proposed changes mailed to interested and affected parties.
Maryland	Copies furnished to licensees, administrative and enforcement officials, trade associations and publications. Hearings are held on proposed Regulations and before adoption must be approved by the Attorney General and filed with the Clerk of the Court of Appeals.
Michigan	Licensees notified by special bulletin; general public, through newspapers and trade journals.
Minnesota	Regulations must be printed once in legal newspaper in St. Paul. Regulations effective 5 days thereafter. Copies must be filed with Secretary of State and with District Courts.
Missouri	Copies to trade associations, trade publications, all parties affected.
Nebraska	Copies of new rules sent to licensees.
Nevada	By letter to licensees, carriers, or holders of certificates of compliance.
New Hampshire	Licensees and permittees provided copy.
New Jersey	Full publicity is given (for benefit of) industry and public.
New Mexico	All interested or affected parties notified 10 days before effective date of regulation.
New York	New rules filed with Secretary of State. Press releases and serialized bulletins inform general public and licensees.
North Carolina	Notification by mail.
North Dakota	(No rule-making power.)
Ohio	Rules affecting public advertised in 3 newspapers, filed with Secretary of State.
Oregon	Copies to all affected licensees. Copies to trade organizations. Public informed through press releases.
Pennsylvania	Notice in newspapers of general circulation and trade publications; occasionally by mail to licensees.
Rhode Island	Notice given in newspaper of general circulation 3 times, last appearing 10 days before effective date.
South Carolina	Affected licensees notified by letter or copy of regulation.
South Dakota	Copies of regulation mailed to affected persons.
Vermont	Copies distributed to all licensees and enforcement officers, and generally an announcement made in newspaper.
Virginia	New regulations must be published at least once in a Richmond paper, and filed with circuit and city court clerks for public inspection.
Washington	All regulations are matters of public record and must be filed in the office of the Secretary of State. Also, whenever a change is made in the regulations, immediate notice is given to the newspapers, and the changes in the regulations are mimeographed and distributed free to all liquor stores and mailed directly to all local officials, to the Liquor Control Board employees, and to those licensees concerned with the change. Every two years a new book containing the Liquor Act and the regulations is printed, and at that time any changes that have been made in the law or the regulations during the interim are incorporated in this book, and it is distributed in the same manner.
West Virginia	No general procedures. Usually affected parties notified of regulation by letter. Beer—notification of state representative of U. S. Brewers Foundation.
Wisconsin	Required to publish once in state paper. Also (unofficially) notify all affected parties by form letter and news stories in newspapers and trade publications.
District of Columbia	Newspaper publication. Notify industry of proposed changes by circular letter.

TABLE 7

SUMMARY OF PROVISIONS IN ABC LAWS COVERING HEARINGS AND APPELLANT PROCEDURES, BY STATES

State	Administrative Hearings				Judicial Review	
	Hearing Agency	Subject Matter of Hearings		Notification and Other Requirements	Right of Appeal	Type of Action
		License Issuance	License Revocation or Suspension			
Alabama	[No statutory provision for hearings, although mention of hearings is made with reference to new application for license.]					
Arizona	Superintendent, Department of Liquor Licenses and Control		X	Reasonable notice required.	Within 10 days to Superior Court.	De novo.
Arkansas	[No administrative hearing, but court appeal.]				Within 20 days to Chancery Court of Pulaski County and then to Supreme Court.	No new evidence heard.
California	State Board of Equalization	X	X	In accordance with California Administrative Practices Act.	To any court of competent jurisdiction in county where person affected resides.	Certiorari.
Colorado	Secretary of State	X	X	Due notice by mail requested.	To any district or county court having jurisdiction of place to be licensed.	Writ of certiorari or otherwise.
Connecticut	Liquor Control Commission.	X	X	10 days' written notice.	Court of Common Pleas, then to Supreme Court of Errors on questions of law.	De novo for beer, but limited on liquor to extent of court's independent investigations.
Delaware	Liquor Commission.	X	X	10 days' notice to applicant and to each person protesting required.	On license application within 10 days to Court of General Sessions of the county where licensee would operate.	De novo.
Florida	Director of State Beverage Department.	X	X	Fair hearing by Director; if he still disapproves, applicant files with County Commissioners and if they then agree with Director, application denied. If County Commissioners disagree with denial by Director, matter sent to Governor who takes final action.	Within 30 days to Circuit Court of county where licensee is to do business.	Writ of certiorari, "or such other remedy as may be appropriate and proper."

TABLE 7—Continued

SUMMARY OF PROVISIONS IN ABC LAWS COVERING HEARINGS AND APPELLANT PROCEDURES, BY STATES

State	Administrative Hearings				Judicial Review	
	Hearing Agency	Subject Matter of Hearings		Notification and Other Requirements	Right of Appeal	Type of Action
		License Issuance	License Revocation or Suspension			
Georgia	State Revenue Commissioner.	[Not required but may conduct hearing]	X			
Idaho	Commissioner of Department of Law Enforcement.	X	X	15 days' notice in writing.	To District Court of county in which licensee resides.	Mandamus by applicant against Commissioner for license issuance or renewal, or injunction for revocation or suspension.
Illinois	Illinois Liquor Control Commission, License Appeal Commission (in Chicago).	X	X	Reasonable notice.	Circuit or Superior Court of county and from these to Supreme Court.	Decision as in civil cases.
Indiana	[No statutory provision for hearings or appeals.]					
Iowa	State Permit Board.		X	Notice of date for hearing to be sent to applicant by registered mail, and hearing to be not less than 7 days from date of mailing notice.		
Kansas Cereal Malt Beverages:	State Commission of Revenue and Taxation and the Director of Revenue		X	Due notice.	District Court of the county, within 20 days.	
Liquor	State Director of Alcoholic Beverage Control.	X	X	Director sets date and place for hearings on applications for retail package store licenses and notifies city or township clerks thereof. Revocation and suspension proceedings in accordance with rules and regulations established by director following reasonable notice to licensee.		

TABLE 7—Continued

SUMMARY OF PROVISIONS IN ABC LAWS COVERING HEARINGS AND APPELLANT PROCEDURES, BY STATES

State	Administrative Hearings				Judicial Review	
	Hearing Agency	Subject Matter of Hearings		Notification and Other Requirements	Right of Appeal	Type of Action
		License Issuance	License Revocation or Suspension			
Kansas—Cont.	Alcoholic Beverage Control Board of Review			Reviews all cases involving appeals from decisions of Director; applicants or licensees must request such review within 15 days following decision of Director.	To District Court of county, thence to State Supreme Court.	
Kentucky	Alcoholic Beverage Control Board or persons designated by the Board	X	X	Applicant has 10 days following license refusal in which to appeal to ABC Board; licensee has 5 days, following decision of State Administrator to revoke license, to appeal to ABC Board.	To Franklin County Circuit Court and from there to Court of Appeals.	Certiorari—Review limited to determining whether or not: (a) Board acted in excess of its powers; (b) order appealed from was procured by fraud; (c) if questions of fact are in issue, whether or not any substantial evidence supports the order appealed from.
Louisiana	Board of Tax Appeals	X	X	Notice by registered mail not less than 5 days and not more than 20 days prior to date of hearing.	To District Court having jurisdiction of the place of business.	De novo.
Maine	State Liquor Commission	X	X	Notice by registered mail 5 days before date set for hearing.		
Maryland	Comptroller and Boards of License Commissioners. State Appeal Board hears cases in a few counties. Appeals may generally be taken, however, from decisions of local licensing authorities				Circuit Court in counties and Baltimore City Court for Baltimore. State Appeal Board hears appeal cases in two counties. No appeals in some cases.	
Massachusetts	Alcoholic Beverages Control Commission	X	X	Due notice.		
Michigan	Liquor Control Commission	X	X	On hearings, notice given by registered mail or in person 4 days prior to hearing.	Proper court.	Writ of certiorari.

90

TABLE 7—Continued

SUMMARY OF PROVISIONS IN ABC LAWS COVERING HEARINGS AND APPELLANT PROCEDURES, BY STATES

State	Administrative Hearings				Judicial Review	
	Hearing Agency	Subject Matter of Hearings		Notification and Other Requirements	Right of Appeal	Type of Action
		License Issuance	License Revocation or Suspension			
Michigan—Cont.				[Public hearings also required twice a year to hear complaints and receive views of public with reference to administration of the Act]	Proper courts.	Writ of certiorari.
Minnesota	[No administrative hearing, but court appeal]				District Court. Either party can appeal to the Supreme Court only on suspension or revocation.	De novo, without a jury.
Mississippi	[No statutory provisions for hearings or appeals]					
Missouri	Supervisor of Liquor Control		X	Licensee may appear of own accord to "protest", at a hearing held for that purpose by the Supervisor.	Circuit Court of County.	De novo, without a jury.
Montana	Montana Liquor Control Board		X	Notice by registered mail not less than 5 days before date of hearing.	To District Court in county within 30 days.	Review by certiorari.
Nebraska	Nebraska Liquor Control Commission	X	X	Reasonable notice.		
Nevada	State Tax Commission	X	X	Reasonable notice of time, place, and subject matter. Hearings held by State Tax Commission before county commissioners.		
New Hampshire	State Liquor Commission		X Suspends without hearing, but can revoke only after hearing	Notice required.		

91

TABLE 7—Continued

SUMMARY OF PROVISIONS IN ABC LAWS COVERING HEARINGS AND APPELLANT PROCEDURES, BY STATES

State	Hearing Agency	Subject Matter of Hearings		Notification and Other Requirements	Right of Appeal	Type of Action
		License Issuance	License Revocation or Suspension			
New Jersey	Commissioner of Alcoholic Beverage Control.	X	X	Notice at least 5 days before hearing.	Appeal from decisions of Commissioner to Appellate Division and Supreme Court of N. J.	De novo unless parties agree to accept record.
New Mexico	[No administrative hearing, but court appeal.]				To District Court of Santa Fe County within 30 days. From District Court to the Supreme Court.	De novo.
New York	[State Liquor Authority.]	X	X	Notice mailed five days before hearing.	To Supreme Court Appellate Division.	Certiorari.
North Carolina	State Board of Alcoholic Control.		X	Notice in writing by registered mail of time and place of hearing. Action by State Board final and not subject to review by any Court.	To Superior Court of the county from adverse decision by local licensing body, but no appeal from action of State Board.	
North Dakota	Attorney General (for liquor).		X	Notice by registered mail, hearing not to be less than 10 days after mailing notice.	To District Court.	De novo, without a jury.
Ohio	Board of Liquor Control.		X	Notice by registered mail.		
Oklahoma	Oklahoma Tax Commission.	X	X	Notice in writing 10 days prior to date of hearing.		
Oregon	[No administrative hearing, but court appeal.]	X			To Circuit Court of county within 10 days of revocation or suspension.	As in equity cases.
Pennsylvania	Pennsylvania Liquor Control Board.	X	X	Notice mailed. Also holds hearings on applications and renewals at times set by it in license districts established by Board.	Court of Quarter Sessions of the county for suspension or revocation.	De novo.

TABLE 7—Continued

SUMMARY OF PROVISIONS IN ABC LAWS COVERING HEARINGS AND APPELLANT PROCEDURES, BY STATES

| State | Administrative Hearings | | | | Judicial Review | |
| | Hearing Agency | Subject Matter of Hearings | | Notification and Other Requirements | Right of Appeal | Type of Action |
		License Issuance	License Revocation or Suspension			
Rhode Island	Liquor Control Administrator or Liquor Control Hearing Board.	X	X	Hear appeals de novo as to law and facts. Notice once a week for at least 2 weeks in paper published in city or town where applicant proposes to carry on business.	Supreme Court within 7 days.	Writ of certiorari.
South Carolina	Tax Commission.		X	Notice by letter 10 days prior to hearing.	Revocation and Suspension: To court of competent jurisdiction of the county for liquor license. To Court of Common Pleas for beer and wine license. For Granting or Refusing to Grant: Reviewable only by Certiorari.	De novo.
South Dakota	Director of Division of Licensing.		X	Due notice, and after hearing put findings of fact in writing as to every alleged violation.	Circuit Court of the county.	Certiorari.
Tennessee	[No provision for administrative hearing, but court appeal.]				Circuit Court of Davidson County, filed within 10 days.	Certiorari
Texas	Texas Liquor Control Board.		X	Notice by registered mail, at least 3 days before date of hearing.	To District Court for refusal or cancellation but not for suspension.	De novo under "same rules as ordinary civil suits."
Utah	Liquor Control Commission.	X	X		No appeal allowed except for contention of fraud.	
Vermont	Vermont Liquor Control Board.		X	Reasonable notice.		
Virginia	Alcoholic Beverage Control Board.	X	X	Notice in writing 10 days prior to hearing.		
Washington	Washington State Liquor Control Board.	X	X	Written notice 5 days prior to hearing.		

TABLE 7—Continued

SUMMARY OF PROVISIONS IN ABC LAWS COVERING HEARINGS AND APPELLANT PROCEDURES, BY STATES

State	Administrative Hearings				Judicial Review	
	Hearing Agency	Subject Matter of Hearings		Notification and Other Requirements	Right of Appeal	Type of Action
		License Issuance	License Revocation or Suspension			
West Virginia	State Tax Commissioner		X	Notice by registered mail 10 days prior to hearing.	Circuit Court of Kanawha County.	Certiorari.
	West Virginia Liquor Control Commission.		X	Notice by registered mail 10 days prior to hearing.	Appropriate court of jurisdiction.	
Wisconsin	[No provision for administrative hearing, but court appeal from local licensing body.]				Any court of record in the respective county.	
Wyoming	Governing bodies of cities, towns, or counties for license renewal hearings.	X (Renewals only.)	X (Renewals only.)	Notice by personal delivery or by posting on premises 10 days prior to hearing in case of license revocation hearings. No special provisions for notice in case of license renewal hearings.	District Court of county in which premises are located for both renewal and revocation hearings.	
	Wyoming Liquor Commission for license revocation hearings.		X			
District of Columbia	Commissioners of the District of Columbia.		X	No provision for notice. Hearing on appeal by licensees in cases where license is revoked or suspended by the ABC Board for period of more than 30 days.		

NOTE: The table is intended only to indicate the types and variety of provisions contained in the ABC laws with respect to administrative hearings and judicial review. Absence of an entry under any particular heading does not necessarily mean that no administrative hearings are held or that there is no possibility of judicial review.

94

TABLE 8

STATUTORY PROVISIONS RELATING TO LICENSING AUTHORITY IN THE REGULATION OF THE RETAIL SALE OF ALCOHOLIC BEVERAGES

PART I—OPEN LICENSE STATES

State	Authority to Issue, Revoke, and Suspend Licenses
Arizona	Licenses issued by Superintendent of Liquor Licenses and Controls after reviewing recommendations of local authorities; Superintendent also suspends or revokes. Local authorities may issue supplementary licenses.
Arkansas	Liquor licenses issued by Commissioner of Revenue; local authorities may issue supplementary licenses. Beer and light wine licenses issued by Commissioner of Revenue and by local authorities; licenses must be obtained from each. Wine licenses issued by Commissioner of Revenue. Commissioner of Revenue suspends or revokes licenses.
California	Licenses issued and suspended or revoked by State Board of Equalization.
Colorado	State licenses issued by Secretary of State, and local jurisdictions require supplementary licenses. Suspension or revocation by courts or Secretary of State for specified violations; mandatory for two or more violations of alcoholic control law.
Connecticut	Licenses issued and suspended or revoked by Liquor Control Commission.
Delaware	Licenses issued and suspended or revoked by Liquor Commission.
Florida	County boards submit recommendations to Director of State Beverage Dept. who approves or disapproves; county boards issue joint state-county, licenses following approval of State Director. State Director, or county board in larger counties, may revoke or suspend. In many instances local governmental units may issue supplementary licenses.
Georgia	Applications for state license must be accompanied by city or county license; State Revenue Commissioner issues, and may revoke or suspend, state licenses, with revocation mandatory for specified offenses.
Illinois	Local authorities issue licenses which are prerequisite to compulsory state licenses; state cannot refuse to license when local licenses have been obtained; local authorities can revoke licenses for violation of ordinances or provisions of the Liquor Control Act.
Indiana	State Commission issues and may revoke licenses; special local boards investigate circumstances of applications and make recommendations theron.
Kansas	Beer licenses issued and revoked by local authorities. Liquor licenses issued and suspended or revoked by Director of Alcoholic Beverage Control.
Kentucky	Alcoholic Beverage Control Board issues and suspends or revokes licenses; local jurisdictions may also issue and suspend or revoke.
Louisiana	State authorities, Collector of Revenue for beer and light wine, and ABC Board for liquor, issue permits, and state authorities may suspend or revoke; local governmental units may issue supplementary licenses and, in the case of beer and light wine licenses, may revoke.
Maryland	Board of Licenses for county (or Baltimore city) has authority to issue and suspend or revoke licenses; in counties not having such boards Clerk of Circuit Court issues, but if there are objections the State Appeal Board issues or denies licenses.
Massachusetts	City or town authorities issue and revoke or suspend licenses in accordance with state provisions; Alcoholic Beverage Control Commission may revoke licenses and review licenses issued by local units for conformity with state provisions.
Minnesota	Local authorities issue and may revoke licenses, but off-sale liquor licenses are subject to approval of, and may be revoked by the Liquor Control Commission.*
Missouri	State Supervision of Liquor Control issues and may revoke licenses; local authorities may issue supplementary licenses.
Nebraska	Commission issues and may suspend or revoke licenses; applications for on-sale licenses in municipalities are submitted through the municipal authorities for recommendation, and municipal authorities may revoke or suspend licenses subject to review of Commission.
Nevada	Local authorities issue and suspend or revoke licenses.
New Jersey	Governing bodies or special boards in larger municipalities issue and may revoke or suspend licenses.
New Mexico	State through Chief of Division of Liquor Control issues and may revoke or suspend licenses; local authorities may issue supplementary licenses.

95

TABLE 8—Continued

STATUTORY PROVISIONS RELATING TO LICENSING AUTHORITY IN THE REGULATION OF THE RETAIL SALE OF ALCOHOLIC BEVERAGES

PART I—OPEN LICENSE STATES

State	Authority to Issue, Revoke, and Suspend Licenses
New York	Local ABC boards accept and investigate all retail license applications and make recommendations to State Liquor Authority; latter issues and may revoke, cancel or suspend any license for cause.
North Dakota	Beer Licenses issued by State Tax Commission; local authorities may issue supplementary licenses; either state or local authorities may suspend or revoke. Liquor licenses issued by both State Attorney General and local authorities and must be obtained from each; either state or local authorities may suspend or revoke.
Rhode Island	Local authorities issue and may revoke or suspend all but certain specified licenses.
South Carolina	State Tax Commission issues and revokes or suspends licenses.
South Dakota	State through Director of Division of Licensing issues licenses following approval by local authorities. State Director may revoke or suspend licenses on own initiative or upon recommendation of local authorities.*
Tennessee	State Commissioner of Finance and Taxation issues off-sale liquor licenses following local certification; and local authorities may issue supplementary licenses; revocation is by State Commissioner. Beer licenses must be obtained from both state and local authorities; local authorities revoke.
Texas	State Liquor Control Board issues and may revoke or suspend licenses; local jurisdictions may issue supplementary licenses.
Wisconsin	Local authorities issue and may suspend or revoke licenses; state may also bring revocation proceedings.*
District of Columbia	Alcoholic Beverage Control Board issues and may revoke or suspend licenses.

* In Minnesota and South Dakota certain municipalities may own and operate stores for the on-sale or off-sale of liquor; Wisconsin authorizes municipal ownership of off-sale stores.

TABLE 8—Continued

STATUTORY PROVISIONS RELATING TO LICENSING AUTHORITY IN THE REGULATION OF THE RETAIL SALE OF ALCOHOLIC BEVERAGES

PART II—MONOPOLY STATES

State	Authority to Issue, Revoke, and Suspend Licenses
Alabama	Beer and on-sale liquor licenses issued by the State Board with the approval of local authorities; Board also revokes and suspends licenses; local authorities may require supplementary licenses.
Idaho	Beer licenses issued by state and by local units with county having final authority; state may revoke beer licenses—action mandatory under certain conditions. On-sale liquor licenses issued and revoked by State Law Enforcement Commissioner; local authorities may require supplementary licenses.
Iowa*	Beer licenses issued and may be revoked by local governmental units in accordance with state provisions; state also issues following issue by local governmental units.
Maine**	Beer and on-sale liquor licenses issued by state following approval by municipal authorities; State Commission may revoke or suspend licenses for specified reasons.
Michigan	On-sale beer, wine, and liquor licenses issued by State Commission following approval by local legislative body (except in Wayne County); revocation is mandatory upon request of local unit or may be revoked or suspended by Commission. Special off-sale beer, wine, and liquor licenses issued in certain cases by State Commission; Commission also revokes.
Montana	Beer and on-sale liquor licenses issued by State Board; Board revokes and suspends licenses for specified reasons; local authorities may issue supplementary licenses.
New Hampshire	On-sale and certain off-sale licenses issued and revoked by State Commission.
North Carolina*	Beer and wine licenses issued by state and local units according to state provisions; issuance obligatory if requirements met; both state and local units may revoke, and revocation of one license cancels other.
Ohio	Beer and on-sale liquor licenses issued and suspended or revoked by Department of Liquor Control.
Oregon*	Beer and wine licenses issued and suspended or revoked by Commission.
Pennsylvania	Beer and on-sale liquor licenses issued and suspended or revoked by Liquor Control Board.
Utah*	Light beer licenses issued and revoked by Liquor Control Commission; local authorities may issue supplementary licenses.
Vermont	On-sale liquor licenses issued and suspended or revoked by State Liquor Board. Beer and wine licenses issued by local authorities following approval by State Liquor Board.
Virginia*	Beer and wine licenses issued and suspended or revoked by State ABC Board. Local authorities may issue supplementary licenses.
Washington*	Beer, wine, and certain on-sale liquor licenses issued and suspended or revoked by Liquor Control Board.
West Virginia*	Beer licenses issued and suspended or revoked by State Tax Commissioner; local authorities may issue supplementary licenses.
Wyoming	Local authorities issue on- and/or off-sale licenses for alcoholic and/or malt beverages; local authorities or State Liquor Commission revokes.

* No sale of liquor by the drink.
** Package liquor may be sold by hotels to bona fide registered guests.

TABLE 9

STATUTORY PROVISIONS OF THE SEVERAL STATES RELATIVE TO THE NUMBER OF ALCOHOLIC BEVERAGE LICENSES WHICH MAY BE ISSUED

No Statutory Provisions

Open License States		Monopoly States
Georgia	Nevada	Alabama
Kansas	North Dakota	Idaho
Louisiana	Oklahoma	Maine
Mississippi	Tennessee	North Carolina
Missouri	Texas	Vermont
		Washington

Discretion Vested in State Authority

Open License States	Monopoly States
Arkansas—Commissioner of Revenue	Montana—State Liquor Control Board
Colorado—Secretary of State	New Hampshire—State Liquor Control Commission
Connecticut—Liquor Control Commission	Oregon—State Liquor Control Commission
Delaware—Delaware Liquor Commission	Virginia—State ABC Board
Kentucky—ABC Board	West Virginia—Beer Commissioner
New Mexico—Chief, Division of Liquor Control	
New York—State Liquor Authority	
South Carolina—South Carolina Tax Commission	
District of Columbia—Commissioners, District of Columbia	

Discretion Vested in Local Authorities

Open License States	Monopoly States
Illinois—Municipal or county legislative bodies	Utah—City, town, or county legislative bodies
Maryland—City or county boards of license commissioners	
Nebraska—City, village, or county legislative bodies	

Numerical Limitation Governs

State	Open License States
Arizona	Hotel and on-sale liquor retailers: counties over 100,000, one for each 2,500; counties 25,000 to 100,000, one for each 2,000; counties less than 25,000 one for each 1,000. Hotel and on-sale beer and wine: one for each 500 inhabitants. Off-sale retailers: same as for hotel and on-sale liquor retailers.
California	Liquor on-sale: one for 1,000 or fraction thereof in each county. Liquor off-sale: one for 1,000 or fraction thereof in each county.
Florida	Liquor licenses limited to one for each 2,500 residents (one for each 1,500 in Miami, Coral Gables, and counties of 45,000-55,000 population) with exception for hotels and certain restaurants and with other exceptions.
Indiana	One liquor retailer permit (including clubs) per 1,000 population for cities and towns, but in counties having two cities of the second class one permit for each 500 population.
Massachusetts	Beer and wine licenses: in towns of 3,000 or less population, four licenses of which not more than three for on-sale and not more than two for off-sale; in towns of 3,001 to 4,001, four licenses of which not more than two for off-sale; in towns of 4,001 to 5,001, five licenses of which not more than two for off-sale; in towns of 5,001 to 15,001, one license for each 1,000 population or fraction thereof, but to include not more than three off-sale licenses; in cities or towns, except Boston, having more than 15,000, one license for each 1,000 or fraction thereof, but to include not more than one off-sale license for each 5,000 or fraction thereof. Other provisions for additional special licenses. Special quotas established for City of Boston.
Minnesota	Limited by various types of cities and towns; however, the limitations, with certain exceptions, in cities of the first class are on-sale license for each 1,500 population.
New Jersey	Discretion vested in the Governing Board of the municipality, except that the number of retail alcoholic beverage seasonal or plenary licenses shall not exceed one for each 1,000 population, or the number of plenary alcoholic beverage licenses shall not exceed one for each 3,000 population providing that any municipality of less than 1,000 population may have one seasonal or plenary retail license.
Rhode Island	Discretion vested in state authority, except that the number authorized cannot exceed the maximum number fixed by local boards and cannot be greater than one for each 1,000 population for on-sale licenses (other than restaurants), one for each 4,000 for restaurant on-sale licenses, and one for each 4,000 population for off-sale licenses and provided that two off-sale licenses may be issued in any town regardless of population.

TABLE 9—Continued

STATUTORY PROVISIONS OF THE SEVERAL STATES RELATIVE TO THE NUMBER OF ALCOHOLIC BEVERAGE LICENSES WHICH MAY BE ISSUED

Numerical Limitation Governs

State	Open License States
South Dakota	In municipalities one on-sale liquor license for each 1,000 population or fraction thereof, except that two licenses may be issued in a municipality of 1,000 population or less; maximum of two off-sale liquor licenses may be issued in a town of 1,000 population or less.
Wisconsin	On-sale liquor licenses limited to one for each 500 inhabitants or fraction thereof.

State	Monopoly States
Iowa	Beer licenses: local authorities authorized to enact limiting ordinances providing that the minimum limitations shall not be less than one for each 500 population up to 2,500 and one for each 750 population for the population over 2,500 with a minimum of two for jurisdictions under 1,000 population; hotels and clubs excluded from these provisions.
Michigan	One on-sale liquor license to each 1,500 population with exceptions for resort areas on seasonal basis and counties having a population of 500,000 or more.
Ohio	Not more than one restaurant on-sale, club on-sale, or night club on-sale and off-sale license may be issued for each 2,000 population.
Pennsylvania	One retail liquor license for each 1,000 inhabitants or fraction thereof in any municipality, exclusive of licenses granted to hotels and clubs.
Wyoming	In local jurisdictions two retail licenses for first 500 population and one additional license for each additional 500 population or major fraction thereof, but not to exceed 20 without special authorization of the State Liquor Commission; Liquor Commission may grant additional licenses upon application of the town councils or boards of county commissioners.

TABLE 10

NUMBER OF OUTLETS PER 1,000 POPULATION RETAILING ANY TYPE OF ALCOHOLIC BEVERAGES—BY STATES AS OF 1945[a]

State	Open License States — No. of Outlets per 1,000 Population				Mean No. of Licenses per 1,000 Population—Monopoly and Private License States Combined	State	Monopoly States — No. of Outlets per 1,000 Population			
	On-Premise	Off-Premise	Combination On- and Off-Premise	Total All Outlets			On-Premise	Off-Premise	Combination On- and Off-Premise	Total All Outlets
Number of Licenses Numerically Restricted						Number of Licenses Numerically Restricted				
Arizona	0.00	0.78	1.65	2.43		Iowa	0.00	0.31	2.34	2.65
California	6.72	1.70	1.32	3.73		Michigan	1.42	1.85	0.08	3.35
Florida	0.78	0.28	3.59	4.65		Ohio	2.05	0.36	0.00	2.41
Indiana	0.20	0.55	1.07	1.82		Pennsylvania	1.95	0.06	0.24	2.25
Massachusetts	1.26	0.88	0.00	2.14		Wyoming	0.00	0.00	0.00	0.00
Minnesota	0.52	0.07	2.20	2.79						
New Jersey	0.14	0.49	2.19	2.82						
Rhode Island	1.63	0.61	0.00	2.24						
South Dakota	0.48	0.97	2.10	3.55						
Wisconsin	0.00	0.80	4.54	5.34						
MEAN	0.57	0.71	1.87	3.15	0.74 0.65 1.42 2.81	MEAN	1.08	0.52	0.53	2.13

No Numerical Restrictions on Number of Licenses

State				Total
Arkansas	1.09	0.60	0.00	1.68
Colorado	0.92	0.65	0.56	2.12
Connecticut	1.83	2.03	0.00	3.86
Delaware	0.49	0.40	0.79	1.69
Georgia	0.00	0.37	2.00	2.37
Illinois	0.00	0.00	2.50[b]	2.50
Kansas	0.00	0.00	1.44	1.44
Kentucky	1.08	0.23	0.07	1.38
Louisiana	1.68	0.43	3.34	5.45
Maryland	0.04	0.47	2.06	2.57
Mississippi	0.00	0.00	2.40	2.40
Missouri	0.00	0.59	1.91	2.50
Nebraska	0.00	0.52	1.71	2.23
Nevada	4.50	0.81	0.00	5.31
New Mexico	1.58	0.32	0.00	1.90
New York	1.76	1.59	0.02	3.37
North Dakota	0.16	0.64	4.09	4.89
Oklahoma	0.00	0.29	1.73	2.02
South Carolina	0.00	0.39	4.44	4.83
Tennessee	0.00	0.13	1.57	1.70
Texas	0.58	0.55	1.02	2.15
District of Columbia	0.81	1.14	0.00	1.94
MEAN	0.75	0.55	1.44	2.74

No Numerical Restrictions on Number of Licenses

State				Total
Alabama	0.12	0.02	0.73	0.87
Idaho	0.00	0.22	3.63	3.85
Maine	0.85	1.79	0.00	2.64
Montana	3.40	0.31	0.00	3.71
New Hampshire	1.73	2.40	0.00	4.13
No. Carolina	0.00	0.44	1.20	1.64
Oregon	0.00	1.60	3.13	4.73
Utah	0.00	0.12	1.77	1.89
Vermont	1.88	2.42	0.00	4.30
Virginia	0.12	0.24	0.95	1.31
Washington	0.23	0.80	1.38	2.41
West Virginia	2.16	0.38	0.00	2.54
MEAN	0.87	0.90	1.07	2.84

| 0.79 | 0.64 | 1.31 | 2.77 |

[a] Source: From data of the various states gathered by the Licensed Beverage Industries, Inc.
[b] Local authorities determine number of on-premise, off-premise, and combination on- and off-premise licenses. No breakdown figures are available, so all licenses are here grouped under combination heading.

TABLE 11

OCCURRENCE IN THE LAWS OF THE SEVERAL STATES OF CERTAIN CRITERIA FOR USE IN SELECTING PERSONS TO BE LICENSED[a]

State	1	2	3	4	5	6	7	8	9	10	11	12	13	Total
Alabama	X	–	X	–	–	X	X	–	–	–	–	–	–	4
Arizona	X	X	X	X	X	–	–	–	–	–	–	–	–	5
Arkansas	X	X	X	X	X	–	–	X	–	–	–	–	–	6
California	X	X	–	X	–	–	X	–	–	–	–	–	–	4
Colorado	X	–	–	–	X	–	–	X	–	X	–	–	–	4
Connecticut	X	–	–	–	–	X	–	X	X	X	X	–	–	6
Delaware	–	X	X	–	X	–	X	–	X	–	X	–	–	6
Florida	–	X	X	X	X	–	X	–	–	X	–	–	–	6
Georgia	–	–	–	–	–	–	–	X	–	–	–	–	–	1
Idaho	X	–	–	X	–	–	–	X	–	–	–	–	–	3
Illinois	X	X	X	X	–	–	–	X	–	X	–	–	–	6
Indiana	–	X	X	–	–	–	–	X	–	–	–	–	–	3
Iowa	X	–	–	X	–	–	–	–	–	–	–	–	–	2
Kansas	X	X	–	X	X	–	X	X	–	X	–	–	–	7
Kentucky	X	X	–	X	X	–	X	–	–	–	–	–	–	5
Louisiana	X	X	X	X	X	–	–	–	–	–	–	–	–	5
Maine	X	–	–	X	X	–	X	–	–	–	–	–	–	4
Maryland	X	–	X	–	X	–	–	X	–	–	–	–	–	4
Massachusetts	X	–	X	–	–	–	–	X	–	X	–	–	–	4
Michigan	X	–	–	X	–	–	–	X	–	X	–	–	–	4
Minnesota	X	–	–	X	X	–	–	–	–	–	–	–	–	3
Missouri	X	–	X	X	–	–	–	X	–	–	–	–	–	4
Montana	X	X	–	X	–	–	–	X	–	–	–	–	–	4
Nebraska	X	X	X	X	–	–	–	X	–	–	–	–	–	5
Nevada	–	–	X	–	–	–	–	–	–	–	–	–	–	1
New Hampshire	X	X	X	–	X	X	X	–	X	–	–	–	–	7
New Jersey	X	X	–	X	X	–	–	X	–	X	–	–	–	6
New Mexico	X	X	–	X	X	X	–	–	–	–	–	–	–	5
New York	X	X	–	X	X	–	X	–	–	X	–	–	–	6
North Carolina	X	X	–	X	X	–	–	X	–	–	–	–	–	5
North Dakota	X	X	–	X	–	–	–	–	–	–	–	–	–	3
Ohio	X	X	–	–	–	–	–	–	–	–	–	–	–	2
Oregon	X	–	–	X	–	–	–	–	X	–	X	–	–	4
Pennsylvania	X	–	X	–	–	–	–	X	–	X	–	–	–	4
Rhode Island	X	–	–	X	–	–	–	X	–	–	–	–	–	3
South Carolina	X	–	X	X	X	–	–	–	–	–	–	–	–	4
South Dakota	X	X	X	–	–	–	X	X	–	–	–	–	–	5
Tennessee	X	X	X	–	X	–	–	X	–	–	–	–	–	5
Texas	–	–	–	X	X	–	X	–	–	–	X	–	–	4
Utah	X	X	X	–	X	–	–	–	–	–	–	–	–	4
Vermont	X	–	–	–	–	–	X	X	–	X	–	–	–	4
Virginia	–	–	–	–	–	–	–	X	–	–	–	–	–	1
Washington	X	X	–	X	–	–	–	X	–	–	–	–	–	4
West Virginia	–	X	X	X	X	–	–	X	–	–	–	–	–	5
Wisconsin	X	X	X	–	–	–	–	X	–	–	–	–	–	4
Wyoming	X	X	X	–	X	–	–	X	–	X	–	–	–	6
District of Columbia	X	X	X	X	X	–	–	–	–	–	–	–	–	5
Total	39	28	23	28	22	4	13	24	4	11	4	0	0	

[a] Based on a table prepared by Licensed Beverage Industries and expanded to include Kansas, Oklahoma Mississippi, and the District of Columbia.
1. Applicant must be a citizen of the United States.
2. Applicant must not have been convicted of a felony.
3. Applicant must be of good repute and moral character.
4. Applicant must not have violated state or federal alcoholic beverage control laws or have had a license revoked during a specified minimum period immediately preceding.
5. Applicant must be of a specified minimum age.
6. Applicant must be a legitimate party in the interest of the place to be licensed.
7. Applicant must not be a party to interlocking industry interests.
8. Applicant must be a resident of the state in which he is applying for a license for a specified minimum period.
9. Applicant must demonstrate adequate financial responsibility.
10. Applicant must not be a licensing or law enforcement official or an employee of any ABC agency.
11. Applicant must not use alcoholic beverages to excess.
12. Applicant must demonstrate ability to read and write.
13. Applicant must demonstrate an understanding of the ABC law and rules.

TABLE 12

OCCURRENCE IN THE LAWS OF THE SEVERAL STATES OF CERTAIN CRITERIA FOR USE IN SELECTING PREMISES TO BE LICENSED [a]

State	Premises Must Be Specified Distance from:				Premises Permitted Only in Areas Not Prohibited by Local Zoning or Other Comparable Local Ordinances	Premises Must Be Open to Full View from Outside or from Entrance	Premises Must Not Open into Connecting Rooms, Buildings or Dwellings [b]
	Schools or Universities	Churches	Hospitals or Institutions	Other Similarly Licensed Outlets			
Alabama	X	—	X	—	—	—	—
Arizona	X	—	—	—	—	—	—
Arkansas	X	X	—	X	—	—	—
California	X	—	X	—	X	—	—
Colorado	X	—	—	—	—	—	—
Connecticut	X	X	X	—	X	X	X
Delaware	X	X	—	—	—	—	—
Florida	X	X	—	—	—	X	X
Georgia	X	X	—	—	X	—	—
Idaho	X	X	—	—	—	—	—
Illinois	X	X	—	—	—	X	X
Indiana	X	X	—	—	—	X	X
Iowa	—	—	—	—	X	—	—
Kansas	X	X	—	—	X	—	X
Kentucky	X	X	X	—	—	X	—
Louisiana	—	—	—	—	—	—	—
Maine	X	X	X	—	—	—	—
Maryland	X	X	—	—	X	X	X
Massachusetts	—	—	—	—	—	—	—
Michigan	—	—	—	—	—	—	—
Minnesota	X	—	—	—	X	X	—
Missouri	X	X	—	—	—	—	X
Montana	X	X	—	—	—	—	—
Nebraska	X	X	X	—	—	X	X
Nevada	—	—	—	—	X	—	—
New Hampshire	—	—	—	—	—	—	—
New Jersey	X	X	—	—	—	—	—
New Mexico	X	X	—	—	—	X	—
New York	X	X	—	X [c]	—	X	—
North Carolina	X	X	—	—	—	—	—
North Dakota	—	—	—	—	—	—	—
Ohio	X	—	—	—	X	X	—
Oregon	—	—	—	—	—	—	—
Pennsylvania	X	X	—	—	—	—	—
Rhode Island	X	X	—	X	—	X	X
South Carolina	—	—	—	—	—	—	—
South Dakota	—	—	—	—	—	X	—
Tennessee	—	—	—	—	X	X	—
Texas	X	X	X	—	X	X	—
Utah	—	—	—	—	—	—	—
Vermont	X	X	—	—	—	—	—
Virginia	—	—	—	—	—	X	—
Washington	X	X	—	—	—	X	—
West Virginia	—	—	—	—	—	—	—
Wisconsin	X	X	X	—	—	X	—
Wyoming	—	—	—	—	—	X	X
Dist. of Columbia	—	—	—	—	X	—	—
Totals	31	25	8	3	12	19	10

[a] Source State Liquor Legislation, prepared by Marketing Laws Survey, U. S. Dept. of Commerce; State Laws and Regulations.
[b] Hotels usually excepted.
[c] As to package stores only.

TABLE 13

REQUIREMENTS FOR PUBLIC NOTICES IN CASES OF APPLICATIONS FOR ALCOHOLIC BEVERAGE LICENSES, BY STATES

State	Original Application			Notice Required for License Renewal
	Notice Required	Notice Not Required	Description of Notice	
Alabama............		X		None
Arizona.............	X		City Clerk posts copy of license application on front of proposed premises 10 days prior to action on application.	None
Arkansas...........	X		Applicant files notice of intent to file in local newspaper.	Same as for original application
California...........	X		Newspaper publication of all on-sale applications. Premise posting. Notice by board to local officials of all applications.	None
Colorado...	X		Applicant posts sign not less than 22″ x 26″ in letters 1″ high, or publishes notice, 1 col. wide and 6″ deep in paper 10 days before approval of application.	None
Connecticut.........	X		Applicant posts placard on door for 3 weeks, and application must be advertised for 2 weeks in local paper.	None
Delaware...........	X		Applicant files ad 3 times, 2 weeks before applying. One ad in paper nearest point of proposed premises.	None
Florida.............		X		None
Georgia.............		X		None
Idaho..............		X		None
Illinois.............	—	—	[Some local issuing authorities require public notice.]	(See under original application)
Indiana.............	X		Notice of license hearing published twice, first publication 15 days before hearing.	Same as for original application
Iowa...............		X		None
Kentucky...........	X		Applicant files ad in county-wide paper once a week for 2 consecutive weeks giving name, address, and proposed site.	None
Louisiana...........	X		Applicants for retail liquor permits must publish notice of application twice in local newspaper.	None
Maine..............	X		Commission publishes notice of license applications in the official state paper for all but off-sale malt liquor licenses.	None
Maryland...........	X		With certain limited exceptions licensing authorities publish notices of license applications 2 times in 2 successive weeks in 3 newspapers. Posting of notices on premises required in some areas.	None
Massachusetts.......	X		Notice published by local issuing authorities in local newspaper, and no action may be taken on licensing until 10 days after publication.	None
Michigan...........	X		Notice required only for club licenses. Notice published once 10 days before license issuance.	None
Minnesota.........		X	State does not require but some municipalities do.	None
Missouri............		X		None
Montana............		X		

104

TABLE 13—Continued

REQUIREMENTS FOR PUBLIC NOTICES IN CASES OF APPLICATIONS FOR ALCOHOLIC BEVERAGE LICENSES, BY STATES

State	Notice Required	Notice Not Required	Description of Notice	Notice Required for License Renewal
			Original Application	
Nebraska............	X		Time and place of license hearing published in paper 3 - 7 days before hearing.	Same as for original application
Nevada.............		X		None
New Hampshire......		X		
New Jersey..........	X		Applicants file ad for publication once a week for 2 weeks.	Same as for original application
New Mexico.........	X		Notice of application posted on proposed premises 20 days before license issuance.	None
New York...........		X a		Same as for original
North Carolina.......	X			None
North Dakota........	X			None
Ohio...............	X			None
Oregon.............	X			None
Pennsylvania.........	X		Notice posted on proposed premises for at least 15 days, beginning day application filed. Posting by applicant.	None
Rhode Island........	X		Notice published in paper by applicant once a week for 2 weeks.	Same as for original application
South Carolina.......	X		Notice published by applicant once a week for 3 weeks in paper of county-wide circulation.	None
South Dakota........	X		Notice required for rural area beer licenses only.	None
Tennessee...........		X		
Texas..............	X		County Clerk posts notice of license application at courthouse door.	None
Utah...............		X		
Vermont.............		X		None
Virginia.............	X		Applicant must post notice on premises and publish once in local paper 10–30 days before application.	None
Washington.........		X	No public notice. Mayor or County Commissioners only are notified of filing.	Same as for original application
West Virginia........		X		None
Wisconsin...........	X		Notice is published on 3 successive days in daily paper or once in weekly paper of locality.	Same as for original application
Wyoming............	X		Town or County Clerk publishes in local newspaper once a week for 4 consecutive weeks notice of license applications and also posts notice of applications on premises.	None
District of Columbia...	X		Must post placard for 2 weeks in conspicuous place on exterior of building. Must publish in newspaper once a week for 2 consecutive weeks in daily paper.	Must post placard for 2 weeks

a New York law requires each licensee to publish a notice of the issuance of his license within 15 days after such issuance.

Source: Questionnaires supplemented by check of respective state laws.

TABLE 14

LICENSE HEARING AND APPEAL PROCEDURES AND ACTIONS AS REPORTED IN QUESTIONNAIRES SUBMITTED BY THE VARIOUS STATES

Procedure for Hearings on License Applications and for Appeals from Decisions of Licensing Authorities

State	Special Comments	By What Method Are Applicants Notified of Hearings?	May All Parties Be Represented by Counsel?	Are Hearings Open to the General Public?	Are Briefs Required?	Are Technical Rules of Evidence Followed?	Is Cross-Examination of Witnesses Permitted?
Alabama		Registered Mail	Yes	Yes	No	No	Yes
Arizona	(Questionnaire not returned)						
Arkansas							
California	Cases are first heard by hearing officer, then by state Board. Applicants may petition Board for rehearing and may also file petition for court review.	Registered Mail	Yes (before Board)	Yes	No	Yes	Yes
Colorado		Mail	Yes	Yes		Yes	Yes
Connecticut		Mail	Yes	Yes	Rarely	Yes	Yes
Delaware		Mail	Yes	Yes	No	Yes	Yes
Florida	Applicants may request a hearing in the event of rejection.		Yes			Yes	Yes
Georgia							
Idaho	No public hearings.						
Illinois	State Commission is appellate body from decisions of local boards (except Chicago).	Mail	Yes	Yes	No	Not strictly	Yes
Indiana		Mail or any other means feasible.	Yes	Yes	No	Not strictly	Yes
Iowa	No hearings by state.						
Kentucky	Hearings are initiated by citation from local administrator to State Board or by citation from State Board itself.	Mail	Yes	Yes	No	Not strictly	Yes
Louisiana	(Questionnaire not returned.)						
Maine	(Questionnaire not returned.)						
Maryland		Mail on applications; police summonses on disciplinary hearings.	Yes	Yes	No	Not strictly	Yes

TABLE 14

LICENSE HEARING AND APPEAL PROCEDURES AND ACTIONS AS REPORTED
IN QUESTIONNAIRES SUBMITTED BY THE VARIOUS STATES

Procedure for Hearings on License Applications and for Appeals from Decisions of
Licensing Authorities

| State | Is a Formal Record of Proceedings Prepared? | Is Record of Proceedings Made Available to the Public? | What Succession of Appeals is Provided For? | Number of Each Type of Hearings Held during Last Completed Fiscal Year | | | | Number of Appeals from Hearings Held during Last Completed Fiscal Year |
				Applications or Renewals	License Disciplinary	Proposed Regulations	Other	
Alabama		Yes		8	48			0
Arizona								
Arkansas				1			3 (transfer of brands)	1 (transfer of brand)
California	Yes	Yes	Appeal from decision of State Board is to appropriate court	486	1,376	2		9
Colorado	Yes	Yes		15	59	0		0
Connecticut	Yes	Yes	Court of Common Pleas; Superior Court of Errors (questions of law only)	520	369			33
Delaware	Yes	No		5	3	0	0	3
Florida	Yes	Yes	Any state court.	0	0			6
Georgia					30			0
Idaho								
Illinois	Yes	Yes					90	4
Indiana	Yes	Yes	Only manufacturers or wholesalers may appeal.		576		450 (informal hearings)	
Iowa								
Kentucky	Yes	Yes	State Board to Circuit Court to Court of Appeals	43	40	6	11	2
Louisiana								
Maine								
Maryland	Yes	Yes	Circuit Courts; State Appeal Board in two counties.	1,237	437			63

TABLE 14—Continued

LICENSE HEARING AND APPEAL PROCEDURES AND ACTIONS AS REPORTED IN QUESTIONNAIRES SUBMITTED BY THE VARIOUS STATES

Procedure for Hearings on License Applications and for Appeals from Decisions of Licensing Authorities

State	Special Comments	By What Method Are Applicants Notified of Hearings?	May All Parties Be Represented by Counsel?	Are Hearings Open to the General Public?	Are Briefs Required?	Are Technical Rules of Evidence Followed?	Is Cross-Examination of Witnesses Permitted?
Massachusetts	(Questionnaire not returned.)						
Michigan	Appeals from Commission decisions may be requested by applicant or attorney.	Mail or wire	Yes	Yes	No	Yes	Yes
Minnesota	No hearings by state. No appeal from decisions of local boards following denial of license. Local and other state hearings informal.						
Missouri	No hearings.						
Montana	(Questionnaire not returned.)						
Nebraska	License applicant may request hearing.	Mail	Yes	Yes	No	Yes	Yes
Nevada			Yes	Public may appear by request			
New Hampshire							
New Jersey	Objectors to license grants may request hearings.		Yes	Yes	No	Yes	Yes
New Mexico	Hearing on applications if requested by local governing bodies; hearings held by State Board.	Mail	Yes	Yes	No	No	Yes
New York	Rejected applicants and objectors to licensing of new premises may call for a hearing.	Mail	Yes	Yes	No	Not strictly	Yes—in discretion of hearing officer.
North Carolina		Mail	Yes		No		
North Dakota		Mail	Yes	Yes	No	Not strictly	Yes
Ohio	Hearings required for permits within 500 ft. of public institutions, or on appeals from action of Director; other hearings at option of Director.	Mail	Yes	Yes	No	Not strictly	Yes

TABLE 14—Continued

LICENSE HEARING AND APPEAL PROCEDURES AND ACTIONS AS REPORTED IN QUESTIONNAIRES SUBMITTED BY THE VARIOUS STATES

Procedure for Hearings on License Applications and for Appeals from Decisions of Licensing Authorities

State	Is a Formal Record of Proceedings Prepared?	Is Record of Proceedings Made Available to the Public?	What Succession of Appeals is Provided For?	Number of Each Type of Hearing Held during Last Completed Fiscal Year				Number of Appeals from Hearings Held during Last Completed Fiscal Year
				Applications or Renewals	License Disciplinary	Proposed Regulations	Other	
Massachusetts								
Michigan	Yes	Yes		235	1,142	0	189	424
Minnesota				0	0	2	1 (label registration)	1
Missouri			From Supervisor to Circuit Court to State Supreme Court	0	404	0		1
Montana								
Nebraska	Yes	No	Rehearing only.	83	66	0		No record.
Nevada	Yes		Board of County Commissioners to State Tax Commission to Courts.			1	1 (penalty on tax payment.)	0
New Hampshire								
New Jersey	Yes	Yes	From local board to State Board to Appellate Court to State Supreme Court	17	192	0	101 (appeals) 48 (seizures) 15 (tax revocations) 3 (petitions)	7
New Mexico	Yes	Yes	From State Board to District Court to State Supreme Court.	1	10	0		2
New York	Yes	Yes	From local board to State board to Appellate Court to Court of Appeals.	4,203	710	No record.	No record.	49 (to Courts).
North Carolina								0
North Dakota	Yes	Yes		0	78	0		8
Ohio	Yes	Yes		279	598	2	4 (statutory 280–500 ft.sec.)	279

TABLE 14—Continued

LICENSE HEARING AND APPEAL PROCEDURES AND ACTIONS AS REPORTED IN QUESTIONNAIRES SUBMITTED BY THE VARIOUS STATES

Procedure for Hearings on License Applications and for Appeals from Decisions of Licensing Authorities

State	Special Comments	By What Method Are Applicants Notified of Hearings?	May All Parties Be Represented by Counsel?	Are Hearings Open to the General Public?	Are Briefs Required?	Are Technical Rules of Evidence Followed?	Is Cross-Examination of Witnesses Permitted?
Oregon	Rejected applicants may request hearings; hearings are informal.	Mail	Yes	Yes	No	No	
Pennsylvania	Rejected applicants may request hearings.	Mail	Yes	Yes	No		Yes
Rhode Island	Remonstrants must be heard by Administrator.	Directly notified	Yes	Yes	Yes—on legal points	Yes—within discretion of Administrator	Yes
South Carolina	Hearings may be held in connection with applications for retail licenses by a hearing officer.	Mail	Yes	Yes	No	No	Yes
South Dakota		Mail					
Tennessee	(Questionnaire not returned.)						
Texas	(Questionnaire not returned.)						
Utah	(Questionnaire not returned.)						
Vermont		Registered Mail	Yes	At discretion of board	No	No	Yes
Virginia	Hearings on license applications held by hearing officer.	Mail	Yes	Yes	No	Not strictly	Yes
Washington	Hearings on license applications in extraordinary cases only.						
West Virginia	No hearings by agency.						
Wisconsin	No hearings procedure prescribed in statutes; governed by each municipality.						
Wyoming	(Questionnaire not returned.)						
District of Columbia	No public hearings held unless there are protests	Mail	Yes	Yes	No	Not strictly	Yes

TABLE 14—Continued

LICENSE HEARING AND APPEAL PROCEDURES AND ACTIONS AS REPORTED
IN QUESTIONNAIRES SUBMITTED BY THE VARIOUS STATES

Procedure for Hearings on License Applications and for Appeals from Decisions of
Licensing Authorities

State	Is a Formal Record of Proceedings Prepared?	Is Record of Proceedings Made Available to the Public?	What Succession of Appeals is Provided For?	Number of Each Type of Hearing Held during Last Completed Fiscal Year				Number of Appeals from Hearings Held during Last Completed Fiscal Year
				Applications or Renewals	License Disciplinary	Proposed Regulations	Other	
Oregon	No			250	240	12	0	1
Pennsylvania	Yes	No	From board to County Court of Quarter Sessions	555	1,019	0	0	496
Rhode Island	Yes	Yes		61	30	10	16 (wholesalers' and retailers' groups)	2
South Carolina	Yes	Yes	Rehearings authorized; no appeal except by certiorari.	100	150	0		0
South Dakota								0
Tennessee							.	
Texas								
Utah								
Vermont	Yes	No		12	28 (represents cases in which action was taken)	2		0
Virginia	Yes	Yes	Rehearing by board. No further appeal.	942	440			0
Washington			No appeal from board.	4	179	0	0	0
West Virginia			Appeals directly to Circuit Court of Kanawha.		30	0		0
Wisconsin								
Wyoming								
District of Columbia	Yes	Yes		53	76	0		2

TABLE 15

STATUTORY AND RULE PROVISIONS RELATING TO LICENSE RENEWAL AND TRANSFER

PART I—NON-MONOPOLY STATES

State	Procedure for Renewal	Procedure for Transfer
Arizona	File renewal applications between Nov. 15 and Dec. 31 or, if seasonal license, not less than 30 days before effective date of renewal; fee must accompany application.	File new application with Superintendent; transferee must be qualified, and be within same county; no transfer may be made if charge is pending, and no transfer as to location unless public convenience is served.
Arkansas	File renewal application before June 30 with proper fee.	Permittee may move to new location providing legal requirements are met; must notify Commissioner of Revenue of change and describe new location; new permit issued.
California	File renewal application with fee on or before date payment due; on-sale retail licenses issued for calendar year, seasonal licenses for fiscal year.	Licenses limited in number may be transferred person to person, or place to place within county—others anywhere in state; reviewed as original application, and new license is subsequently issued.
Colorado	File renewal application with fee on or before Dec. 1, renewal considered as new application.	Application for transfer of place to Secretary of State; transfer may be within city, town, or county for which originally issued; must be approved by Secretary of State and local licensing authority.
Connecticut	File renewal application in same manner as original application; must file 21 days before expiration date.	Licensees may move from premise to premise following endorsement by Liquor Control Commission; new permittees may be substituted for former permittees provided original licensing requirements are met.
Delaware	File renewal application before Mar. 31; decision of Commission must be made before June 1.	Licenses may be transferred to any person subject to approval of the Commission.
Florida	License renewable upon payment of fee to tax collector before Oct. 1.	Licenses transferable to a bona fide purchaser of the business, provided qualifications for license are met and transfer approved by the Commissioner; transfer to another location within same town or city accomplished by surrendering old license and applying for new to be approved by County Commission and State Director.
Georgia	Licenses are renewable upon payment of fees annually under Malt Beverage Law; wine and wholesaler licenses expire on Dec. 31; license fees under Liquor Control Act are payable in advance on or before Jan. 1.	Transfer from location to location upon approval of local, city, or county authorities and by the Commissioner of Revenue.
Illinois	Licenses are renewable at expiration but licensee and premises must be qualified; renewal privilege not a vested right.	Transfer to new location upon approval by Commissioner and local authorities; new premises must meet specifications.
Indiana	No statutory provisions for renewal of retail permits.	Transfer from person to person. location to location permitted providing unexpired portion of license is 3 or more months; application for transfer considered as new application.
Kansas	Liquor licenses renewable one year from date of issue; beer licenses issued for calendar year and renewable at end of calendar year.	Transfer of liquor licenses to new premises authorized provided such premises meet new license requirements; no transfer of retail beer licenses.
Kentucky	No statutory provisions for renewal.	All transfers must be approved by the State Administrator; assignment to receivers must be endorsed by Administrator.
Louisiana	File application annually on or before Nov. 1, with proper fee; penalty of 5% of fee for failure to file each month after Nov. 1 up to Dec. 31 when license may be suspended without notice or hearing.	In person to person transfer, transferee must apply for and pay fee attending a new license; changes in location must be noted on license by issuing authority, and license is not valid until such change is made.

TABLE 15—Continued

STATUTORY AND RULE PROVISIONS RELATING TO LICENSE RENEWAL AND TRANSFER

PART I—NON-MONOPOLY STATES

State	Procedure for Renewal	Procedure for Transfer
Maryland	File application certifying that facts in original application are unchanged, accompanied by statement of approval of renewal by owner of premises and proper fee, applications for renewal in Harford County subject to rules of Liquor Board; statement of renewal approval by owner not required in Pr. Georges County if applicant holds lease upon entire building for a period not less than the term of the renewal; hearing held if renewal protested.	New location and/or assignee must be approved before transfer is affected; no transfer of any kind in Allegany County; bulk sale license must be acquired for sale of stock.
Massachusetts	Holders of annual license who apply in November or holders of seasonal licenses who apply in March are prima facie entitled to same type license if quota is larger than number of renewal applications; licenses are re-issued in order of their application; local authorities must approve premises for on-sale license renewals; dry vote does not affect renewal of wholesaler or importer licenses.	Transfer to new location subject to approval by local and state authorities; transfer between persons may be approved by licensing authorities if in the public interest.
Minnesota	Local licenses may be renewed upon payment of fee and filing application as for original issuance; no specific provisions for renewal of state licenses.	Licenses may be transferred from person to person and from premise to premise subject to the approval of the Liquor Control Commission and/or the respective issuing authority or municipal council.
Missouri	Application for renewal to be submitted to district liquor control office before May 1 with proper fee.	License of deceased licensee may be transferred to next of kin upon application to and approval by, the Supervisor of Liquor Control.
Nebraska	Application for renewal approved providing licensee is qualified and premises are suitable for the purpose.	Licenses are not transferable (A. G. opin.).
Nevada	Licenses are renewable upon payment of proper fee but no statutory provisions on renewal procedures.	Licenses are not transferable.
New Jersey	Licenses are renewable upon application and payment of fee to proper issuing authority.	Licenses transferable as to location or as to person by publication of notice of intent to transfer, payment of fee, endorsement of transferor, and approval by the issuing authority; licenses may be transferred for the unexpired term to an executor, administrator, trustee, receiver, or other person by the Liquor Commissioner in event of bankruptcy, death, or receivership of licensee.
New Mexico	All existing licensees in good standing are entitled to renewal upon payment of annual fee.	For transfer between persons, transferee must furnish bond and pay fee with the application; for transfer to new locations licensee must post notice of intent at the proposed new premises for 20 days, and approval of local authorities in the district of the new premises be obtained.
New York	Application for renewal must be made but certain information may be waived. Fee paid at time of application. Affidavit in lieu of photo of premises permitted.	Licenses are not transferable.
North Dakota	No statutory provisions relating to renewal.	Transfer of premises may be made within same town, village, or city subject to approval of local board and authorization by the state (A. G. opin.); beer permits are not transferable.

TABLE 15—Continued

STATUTORY AND RULE PROVISIONS RELATING TO LICENSE RENEWAL AND TRANSFER

PART I—NON-MONOPOLY STATES

State	Procedure for Renewal	Procedure for Transfer
Rhode Island	Off-sale retail licenses are renewable upon application and payment of fee and are prima facie entitled to renewal, but application may be rejected for cause; hearing if reapplication refused for cause.	Transfer may be made between persons or locations upon application and posting new bond as in the case of an original application; public notice must also be given.
South Carolina	No statutory provisions for renewal.	Personal representative of a deceased retail or wholesale licensee may carry on business with approval of tax Commission and Probate Court.
South Dakota	No statutory provisions for renewal.	Transfer applications are treated as original applications; written statement that bulk sales are conditional upon grant of license required in person to person transfers; application for transfer to new location must include pertinent facts relating to the new premises; all rights of license succeed to the personal representative of a deceased licensee except Class G (solicitor) and Class L (non-beverage alcohol) licenses.
Tennessee	Renewal may be made by application accompanied by a certificate of good moral character issued by the County Judge, Mayor, or Council; application must also be accompanied by fee.	Transfer to a new location may be made upon written request to the Commissioner, showing reason for transfer and approved by the local official; transfer may be denied in the public interest (regulation); transfer of beer license with the business may be made when business is to be conducted at the same location; transferee must execute regular bond (A. G. opin.).
Texas	Liquor licenses renewable as of Aug. 31 each year; beer licenses expire one year from date of issue.	Licenses may be transferred from premises to premises upon application to, and approval of, county judge; no transfer of licenses from person to person authorized.
Wisconsin	No statutory provisions for renewal.	Transfer may be made to new location in the same municipality only once in the same year. Survivor, administrator, trustee or receiver may transfer license to a fully qualified person with consent of authority.
District of Columbia	Application to the Board and payment of fee by January 15.	Transfer to new premises or other person may be made upon application to the Board and hearing in same manner as for a new license.

TABLE 15

STATUTORY AND RULE PROVISIONS RELATING TO LICENSE RENEWAL AND TRANSFER

PART II—MONOPOLY STATES

State	Procedure for Renewal	Procedure for Transfer
Alabama	Applications for renewal must be filed 60 days prior to expiration, and, unless objections are filed within one month after such filing, applicant is entitled to renewal upon payment of fee; hearing held if objection is filed.	Transfers to another person or location may be made only within the same municipality if the person or place is fully eligible; license terminates upon insolvency or bankruptcy.
Idaho	No statutory provisions for renewal.	Statutes require separate licenses for retailer and premises; beer licenses may be transferred to another person provided all qualifications of character, etc., are met; liquor-by-the-drink licenses may be transferred to a guardian, executor, receiver, trustee or assignor upon written permission of the Commissioner.
Iowa	No statutory provisions for renewal.	Permits are not transferable nor assignable; new permit applications must be filed in the event of any change in lincensee or premises.
Maine	No statutory provisions for renewal.	Transfer of on-sale licenses of hotels, clubs, and restaurants to a new location upon written application and approval by the Commission, providing new premises must meet all requirements; transfer to executor administrator, or trustee may be made with approval of municipal officials subject to the descretion of the commission for a period not to exceed 6 months; licenses may not be transferred under any other condition.
Michigan	No statutory provisions for renewa .	Licenses may be transferred with the consent of the Liquor Control Commission; local authorities must approve on-sale license transfers.
Montana	No statutory provisions for renewal.	Transfer of retail beer or retail liquor licenses may be made with the approval of the State Liquor Control Board by application; original licensee makes application.
New Hampshire	No statutory provisions for renewal.	Licenses may not be transferred without the written consent of the Liquor Commission.
North Carolina	No statutory provisions for renewal.	County beer and wine license may be transferred to a new location upon approval of amended license by the County Commissioner (A.G. opin.).
Ohio	Applications for reissue filed with the Liquor Control Dept. not less than 15 days prior to expiration.	Transfer to a new location subject to approval of Liquor Control Dept.; transfer of permits to another person may be made at the discretion of the Director of Liquor Control in cases of death, bankruptcy, etc., to the legal executor or receiver, or, in cases of sale of a business (as a result of undue hardship) upon evidence that the purchaser can meet all qualifications for permittee.
Oregon	Application made to the Commission.	The Liquor Control Commission has discretion to approve the transfer of any license; the business of any insolvent or deceased licensee may be operated by another at the discretion of the Commission for the unexpired term of the license.
Pennsylvania	Application to the Board 60 days before expiration date with filing fee of $10 plus license fee; hearing if objections filed ten days before renewal time.	Transfers between persons or to new premises may be made if the transferee and premises meet all qualifications for license; execution of bond required; appeal to courts provided upon refusal of Board to transfer; license may also be transferred upon death of licensee to survivor approved by the Board; licenses are cancelled in cases of bankruptcy.
Utah	No statutory provisions for renewal.	No statutory provisions relating to transfer of retail licenses.

115

TABLE 15—Continued

STATUTORY AND RULE PROVISIONS RELATING TO LICENSE RENEWAL AND TRANSFER

State	Procedure for Renewal	Procedure for Transfer
Vermont...........	Licenses may be renewed upon application and payment of fee to the Board.	Transfer of license to a new location upon application to, and amendment of the license by, the Liquor Control Board; licenses may be transferred by the Board upon death of the licensee to the administrator or executor until expiration of the license.
Virginia............	No statutory provisions for renewal.	Licenses under light beer law may be transferred to new premises within the same city or county; licenses under alcoholic beverages law may be transferred anywhere within the state; publication of notice required if not in the same county or city; licenses may not be transferred to another person; special permit, not to exceed unexpired term of license, may be obtained to operate premises upon death of licensee.
Washington........	No statutory provisions for renewal.	Transfer to another person may be made by application by both parties to the Board for approval; changes in location may be made upon application by licensee; evidence of qualification must be provided in either case.
West Virginia.......	No statutory provisions for renewal.	With the approval of the Commission licenses may be amended to change the location of premises; otherwise, licenses are not transferable.
Wyoming..........	Upon expiration, the owner shall have preference right to renewal.	Licenses may be sold providing bona fide sale is made and transferee makes application to the Commission and approval is given by local licensing body; transfer as to premises may be made in special cases and upon satisfaction of new license requirements.

TABLE 16

OCCURRENCE IN THE LAWS OF THE SEVERAL STATES OF SPECIFIC PROVISIONS RELATING TO THE TRANSFER OF ALCOHOLIC BEVERAGE RETAIL LICENSES TO NEW PERSONS AND TO NEW PREMISES

State	May Licenses Be Transferred from Person to Person?[a]	May Licenses Be Transferred from Premises to Premises?	Does Law State That Transfers between Persons Are Subject to Same Qualifications as New Licenses?	Does Law State That Transfers between Premises Are Subject to Same Qualifications as New Licenses?
Alabama	Yes	Yes	Yes	Yes
Arizona	Yes	Yes	Yes	Yes
Arkansas	No	Yes	—	Yes
California	Yes	Yes	Yes	Yes
Colorado	No	Yes	—	—
Connecticut	Yes	Yes	Yes	—
Delaware	Yes	—	—	—
Florida	Yes	Yes	Yes	Yes
Georgia	No	Yes[b]	—	—
Idaho	Yes	Yes	Yes	—
Illinois	No	Yes	—	Yes
Indiana	Yes	Yes	Yes	Yes
Iowa	No	No	—	—
Kansas	Liquor: No Malt beverages: No	Liquor: Yes Malt beverages: No	—	Yes
Kentucky	By consent of licensing authority		—	—
Louisiana	Yes	Yes	Yes	—
Maine	No	Yes	—	Yes
Maryland	Yes	Yes	Yes	Yes
Massachusetts	By consent of licensing authority		—	—
Michigan	By consent of licensing authority		—	—
Minnesota	By consent of licensing authority		—	—
Missouri	No	No	—	—
Montana	By consent of licensing authority		—	—
Nebraska	No	No	—	—
Nevada	No	No	—	—
New Hampshire	By consent of licensing authority		—	—
New Jersey	Yes	Yes	Yes	—
New Mexico	Yes	Yes	Yes	—
New York	No	Yes	—	—
North Carolina	—	Yes[b]	—	—
North Dakota	No	By consent of licensing authority[b]	—	—
Ohio	Special cases only	Yes	—	—
Oregon	By consent of licensing authority		—	—
Pennsylvania	Yes	Yes	Yes	Yes
Rhode Island	Yes	Yes	Yes	Yes
South Carolina	No	—	—	—
South Dakota	Yes	Yes	Yes	Yes
Tennessee	Liquor: No Beer: Yes	Liquor: Yes Beer: No	—	—
Texas	No	Yes	—	—
Utah	—	—	—	—
Vermont	No	Yes	—	—
Virginia	No	Yes	—	—
Washington	Yes	Yes	—	—
West Virginia	No	Yes	—	—
Wisconsin	No	Yes	—	—
Wyoming	Yes	Special cases only	Yes	Yes
District of Columbia	Yes	Yes	Yes	Yes

[a] The majority of state ABC laws permit transfers of licenses to executors or administrators upon the death of licensees. Where only this type of license transfer is authorized a negative answer is entered in the column below.

[b] Attorney General's Opinion.

TABLE 17

PROVISIONS IN THE LAWS OF THE SEVERAL STATES RELATIVE TO THE RENEWAL OF ALCOHOLIC BEVERAGE RETAIL LICENSES

State	Term of Licenses	Do Licenses Generally Expire on the Same Date?	How Many Days Prior to Expiration of Old License Does Law Require Filing of Renewal Application?	Does Law State that Renewals Are Subject to Same Qualifications for Persons and Premises as Initial Applications?
Alabama............	1 year	Yes	60	—
Arizona.............	1 year	Yes	1 to 45	—
Arkansas...........	1 year	Yes	—	—
California...........	1 year	Yes	—	—
Colorado...........	1 year	Yes	30 or more	—
Connecticut.........	1 year	No	21	Yes
Delaware...........	1 year	Yes	60	—
Florida.............	1 year	Yes	—	—
Georgia............	1 year	Liquor: Yes Beer: No	—	—
Idaho..............	1 year	Yes	—	—
Illinois.............	1 year	Yes	—	Yes
Indiana.............	1 year	Yes	—	—
Iowa...............	1 year	Liquor: Yes Beer: No	—	—
Kansas.............	1 year	Liquor: No Malt beverages: Yes	—	Liquor: Yes Malt beverages: —
Kentucky...........	1 year	Yes	—	—
Louisiana...........	1 year	Yes	60	—
Maine..............	1 year	Yes	—	—
Maryland...........	1 year	Yes	30 to 60	Yes
Massachusetts.......	1 year	Yes	—	Yes
Michigan...........	1 year	Yes	—	—
Minnesota..........	1 year	No[a]	—	Yes
Missouri............	1 year	Yes	60	—
Montana............	1 year	Yes	—	—
Nebraska...........	1 year	Yes	—	Yes
Nevada............	1 year	Yes	—	—
New Hampshire......	1 year	Yes	—	—
New Jersey.........	1 year	Yes	—	—
New Mexico........	1 year	Yes	—	Yes
New York...........	1 year	No[a]	—	Yes
North Carolina......	1 year	Yes	—	—
North Dakota.......	1 year	Yes	—	—
Ohio...............	1 year	No	15 or more	—
Oregon.............	1 year	Yes	—	Yes
Pennsylvania........	1 year	No[a]	60	Yes
Rhode Island........	1 year	Yes	—	—
South Carolina......	1 year	Yes	—	—
South Dakota.......	1 year	Yes	—	—
Tennessee..........	1 year	Yes	—	—
Texas..............	1 year	Liquor: Yes Wine & beer: No	Liquor: — Wine & beer: 5 to 30	Yes
Utah...............	1 year	Yes	—	—
Vermont............	1 year	Yes	—	Yes
Virginia............	1 year	Yes	—	—
Washington.........	1 year	Yes	—	—
West Virginia.......	1 year	Yes	—	—
Wisconsin..........	1 year	Yes	—	—
Wyoming...........	1 year	No	—	—
District of Columbia...	1 year	Yes	—	—

[a] Licenses in particular districts or local jurisdictions expire on same date, but there is no set license year for entire state.

TABLE 18

STATUTORY PROVISIONS GOVERNING THE ASSIGNMENT OF ENFORCEMENT RESPONSIBILITIES TO STATE AND LOCAL UNITS

State	Location of Basic Responsibility for Enforcement of ABC Laws	Location of Responsibility for Detecting ABC Law Violations	Location of Responsibility for Prosecuting ABC Law Violators	Location of Responsibility for Suspending or Revoking ABC Licenses	Body to Which Appeals in Cases of Suspension or Revocation May Be Taken
Alabama	Not specifically delegated; presumably vested in ABC Board.	State and local law enforcement authorities and agents of the ABC Board.	No statutory provisions.	ABC Board.	Presumably no appeal may be taken.
Arizona	Superintendent of Liquor Licenses and Control.	Agents of the Dept. of Liquor Licenses and Control.	No statutory provisions.	Superintendent of Liquor Licenses and Controls.	County Superior Court.
Arkansas	Commissioner of Revenues and his deputies and employees, and local law enforcement authorities.	Commissioner of Revenues jointly with prosecuting attorneys, sheriffs, and other law-enforcing officers of the state for beer and wine laws; circuit judges and state and local police officers for general enforcement of liquor laws.	Prosecuting attorneys.	Commissioner of Revenues.	Chancery Court of Pulaski County.
California	Not specifically delegated; presumably vested in State Board of Equalization.	Agents of the Board of Equalization and all peace officers and district attorneys.	District attorneys.	State Board of Equalization.	Any court of competent jurisdiction in county in which licensee resides.
Colorado	State Licensing Authority (Secretary of State) and local law enforcement officers.	Local police officers and district attorneys, and every police or peace officer.	No statutory provisions.	State Licensing Authority and local legislative bodies or licensing authorities.	No statutory provisions.
Connecticut	Liquor Control Commission.	Agents of Liquor Control Commission and local peace officers.	State's Attorney, prosecuting attorneys of criminal courts or local prosecuting officers and all grand juries.	Liquor Control Commission.	Court of Common Pleas.
Delaware	Liquor Control Commission.	Liquor Control Commission assisted by peace officers, sheriffs, grand juries, and the Attorney General.	State's Attorney.	Liquor Control Commission.	No appeal may be taken (Delaware Supreme Court Decision).
Florida	Governor, Director of the State Beverage Dept., and supervisors appointed by the Governor.	Department supervisors and county sheriffs.	No statutory provisions.	Director of State Beverage Dept. and certain county boards.	Circuit court of county in which revocation took place.
Georgia	State Revenue Commissioner.	Agents of State Revenue Commissioner, sheriffs, and other peace officers.	Solicitor General of the state or county prosecuting officer.	State Revenue Commissioner and local issuing authorities.	No statutory provisions.
Idaho	Not specifically delegated; presumably vested in Commissioner of Law Enforcement.	Sheriffs and local peace officers, and agents of the Commissioner of Law Enforcement.	County prosecuting attorneys and the State's Attorney General.	Commissioner of Law Enforcement.	District court of county in which licensee resides.

TABLE 18—Continued

STATUTORY PROVISIONS GOVERNING THE ASSIGNMENT OF ENFORCEMENT RESPONSIBILITIES TO STATE AND LOCAL UNITS

State	Location of Basic Responsibility for Enforcement of ABC Laws	Location of Responsibility for Detecting ABC Law Violations	Location of Responsibility for Prosecuting ABC Law Violators	Location of Responsibility for Suspending or Revoking ABC Licenses	Body to Which Appeals in Cases of Suspension or Revocation May Be Taken
Illinois	Not specifically delegated; presumably vested in various local liquor control commissions and in State Liquor Control Commission.	Officers and employees of the Revenue Dept. and local police officials.	No statutory provisions.	Local liquor control commissions and, under certain conditions, the State Liquor Control Commission.	State Liquor Control Commission or a city license appeal commission; thence to County Circuit Court or Superior Court.
Indiana	Alcoholic Beverage Commission.	Deputies of the Alcoholic Beverage Commission and, by implication, all police officers.	Prosecutor of the Indiana Beverage Commission.	Alcoholic Beverage Commission.	No appeal may be taken.
Iowa	County attorneys.	County attorneys assisted by sheriffs and their deputies; the police officers of every city and town; and the State Dept. of Public Safety.	County attorneys.	Local governmental units.	No statutory provisions.
Kansas	Liquor; State Director of Alcoholic Beverage Control. Beer: not specifically delegated; presumably vested in respective local licensing officials.	Liquor: officers, agents, and employees of Director of Alcoholic Beverage Control. Beer: sheriffs and deputies, constables, mayors, marshals, police judges, and police officials.	Liquor: county attorneys. Beer: city and county attorneys.	Liquor: State Director of Alcoholic Beverage Control. Beer: local licensing authorities.	Liquor: Alcoholic Beverage Control Board, thence district courts. Beer: district courts.
Kentucky	Not specifically delegated; presumably vested in State Alcoholic Beverage Control Board.	Representatives of State Alcoholic Beverage Control Board and peace officers.	No statutory provisions.	State Alcoholic Beverage Control Board and city and county administrators.	Franklin County Circuit Court.
Louisiana	Board of Alcoholic Beverage Control.	Board of Alcoholic Beverage Control, municipal authorities, and sheriffs.	No statutory provisions.	Board of Alcoholic Beverage Control.	District courts having jurisdiction.
Maine	Not specifically delegated; presumably vested in State Liquor Commission.	Agents of the State Liquor Commission, mayors, aldermen, assessors, and constables.	County attorneys and, in some instances, the State's Attorney General.	State Liquor Commission.	No statutory provisions.
Maryland	State's Attorneys, sheriffs, constables, bailiffs, police, and other peace officers; Comptroller and Local Boards.	State's Attorneys, sheriffs, constables, bailiffs, police, and other peace officers.	State's Attorneys and all other prosecuting officers.	State Comptroller, Board of License Commissioners for any county or Baltimore City, or State Appeal Board.	County circuit courts or Baltimore City Court; State Appeal Board in two counties.
Massachusetts	Not specifically delegated; presumably vested in local licensing authorities and State Alcoholic Beverages Control Commission.	State and local police officers.	No statutory provisions.	State Alcoholic Beverages Control Commission or local licensing authorities.	State Alcoholic Beverages Control Commission (Decision is final).
Michigan	County sheriffs, village marshals, constables, officers or members of village or city police; state police; and inspectors of Commission.	County sheriffs and deputies, village law enforcement officers, city police, and inspectors of the Commission.	No statutory provisions.	Liquor Control Commission.[a]	Appropriate court by writ of certiorari.

TABLE 18—Continued

STATUTORY PROVISIONS GOVERNING THE ASSIGNMENT OF ENFORCEMENT RESPONSIBILITIES TO STATE AND LOCAL UNITS

State	Location of Basic Responsibility for Enforcement of ABC Laws	Location of Responsibility for Detecting ABC Law Violations	Location of Responsibility for Prosecuting ABC Law Violators	Location of Responsibility for Suspending or Revoking ABC Licenses	Body to Which Appeals in Cases of Suspension or Revocation May Be Taken
Minnesota	Not specifically delegated; presumably vested in local authorities.	Local police officers and agents of Liquor Control Commission.	No statutory provisions.	Respective issuing authorities and Liquor Control Commissioner.	District court of county in which place of business is maintained.
Missouri	Prosecuting attorneys of various counties, circuit attorneys, and the Attorney General.	Prosecuting attorneys, circuit attorneys, the Attorney General, and the Supervisor of Liquor Control and his agents.	County prosecuting attorneys, circuit attorneys, and, in some cases, the Attorney General.	Supervisor of Liquor Control.	Circuit court of county in which licensee is located.
Montana	Not specifically delegated; presumably vested in State Liquor Control Board.	Any sheriff, police officer, or inspector appointed under the Liquor Control Act.	County Attorney or State's Attorney General.	State Liquor Control Board.	District court of county of residence.
Nebraska	Liquor Control Commission assisted by other administrative departments of the state, county, and municipal governments; all peace officers; and prosecuting officers.	Local police officers and inspectors of the Liquor Control Commission.	No statutory provisions.	Local issuing authorities and Liquor Control Commission.	Liquor Control Commission in case of revocation by local authorities (no further appeals).
Nevada	Not specifically delegated; presumably vested in State Tax Commission.	Sheriffs, local police officers, and agents of the State Tax Commission.	No statutory provisions.	State Tax Commission on recommendation of boards of county commissioners.	No statutory provisions.
New Hampshire	Not specifically delegated; presumably vested in State Liquor Commission.	State Liquor Commission and its agents and police officers of cities and towns.	Agents of the State Liquor Commission.	State Liquor Commission.	No statutory provisions.
New Jersey	State Commissioner of Alcoholic Beverage Control.	Inspectors and investigators of the State Commission and all police officers in the state.	No statutory provisions.	State Commissioner of Alcoholic Beverage Control or respective local issuing authorities.	State Commissioner of Alcoholic Beverage Control, thence to Appellate Division.
New Mexico	Not specifically delegated; presumably vested in Chief of Division of Liquor Control.	Agents of Liquor Control Division and local police officers.	No statutory provisions.	Chief of Division of Liquor Control.	District Court of Santa Fe County.
New York	Criminal: All local law enforcement officers. Administrative: State Liquor Authority.	All local law enforcement officers.	Criminal: District Attorneys Administrative: State Liquor Authority.	State Liquor Authority.	State Supreme Court, Appellate Division; then Court of Appeals.
North Carolina	State Alcoholic Control Board and various county boards.	Local police officers and enforcement officers of the county control Boards.	County and State's Attorneys.	Governing boards of municipalities, boards of county commissioners, State Commissioner of Revenue, and State Board of Alcoholic Control.	Superior Court or municipal or county court having jurisdiction.[b]

TABLE 18—Continued

STATUTORY PROVISIONS GOVERNING THE ASSIGNMENT OF ENFORCEMENT RESPONSIBILITIES TO STATE AND LOCAL UNITS

State	Location of Basic Responsibility for Enforcement of ABC Laws	Location of Responsibility for Detecting ABC Law Violations	Location of Responsibility for Prosecuting ABC Law Violators	Location of Responsibility for Suspending or Revoking ABC Licenses	Body to Which Appeals in Cases of Suspension or Revocation May Be Taken
North Dakota	The Attorney General, his inspectors, and all peace officers.	Inspectors appointed by the Attorney General and all peace officers.	State's Attorney.	Attorney General, State Tax Commissioner, or governing bodies of local issuing jurisdiction.	District court having jurisdiction.
Ohio	Dept. of Liquor Control.	Department inspectors and state and local police officers.	No statutory provisions.	Board of Liquor Control.	No appeal may be taken.
Oregon	State police and local law enforcement officers; also, presumably, the Liquor Control Commission.	Inspectors and investigators of the Liquor Control Commission and police officers of local jurisdictions.	No statutory provisions.	Liquor Control Commission.	Circuit court of county of residence.
Pennsylvania	Not specifically delegated; presumably vested in Liquor Control Board.	Enforcement officers of the Liquor Control Board.	No statutory provisions.	Liquor Control Board.	Court of quarter sessions of county in which premise is located.
Rhode Island	Director of Business Regulation and local sheriffs, police, and other law enforcement authorities.	Agents of the Director of Business Regulation and local sheriffs, police, and other law enforcement authorities.	No statutory provisions.	Various local licensing authorities and Dept. of Business Regulation.	Liquor Control Administrator or Liquor Control Hearing Board, thence State Supreme Court.
South Carolina	Not specifically delegated; presumably vested in State Tax Commission.	Agents of State Tax Commission, state constabulary, and local police officers.	No statutory provisions.	State Tax Commission.	Any court of competent jurisdiction for liquor license appeals; court of common pleas in county of residence for beer and wine license appeals.
South Dakota	Not specifically delegated; presumably vested in Director of Division of Licensing.	State inspectors and local police officers.	No statutory provisions.	Director of Division of Licensing.	Circuit court of county in which premises are operated.
Tennessee	Commissioner of Finance and Taxation assisted by grand juries of the state, sheriffs, and other peace officers of the state, its cities, and counties.	State and local police, and inspectors of the Dept. of Agriculture.	No statutory provisions.	Commissioner of Finance and Taxation and municipal authorities in case of beer licensees under their jurisdiction.	Circuit Court of Davidson County for liquor licensees; circuit court of county in which premises are located for beer licensees.
Texas	State Liquor Control Board assisted by city, county, and state peace officers.	Inspectors and representatives of the State Liquor Control Board and local peace officers.	Assistant Attorneys General assigned to State Liquor Control Board.	State Liquor Control Board or Liquor Control Administrator.	District court of county in which premises are located.
Utah	Inspectors of the State Liquor Control Commission; all local police; prosecuting and executive officers.	Inspectors of the State Liquor Control Commission; all local police; prosecuting and executive officers.	Any public prosecuting attorney.	State Liquor Control Commission.	No appeal may be taken except for contention of fraud.

TABLE 18—Continued

STATUTORY PROVISIONS GOVERNING THE ASSIGNMENT OF ENFORCEMENT RESPONSIBILITIES TO STATE AND LOCAL UNITS

State	Location of Basic Responsibility for Enforcement of ABC Laws	Location of Responsibility for Detecting ABC Law Violations	Location of Responsibility for Prosecuting ABC Law Violators	Location of Responsibility for Suspending or Revoking ABC Licenses	Body to Which Appeals in Cases of Suspension or Revocation May Be Taken
Vermont	Liquor Control Board in collaboration with local police officers and sheriffs.	Inspectors of the Liquor Control Board and local police officers and sheriffs.	State's Attorney or any town grand juror.	Liquor Control Board or local control commissioners.	No statutory provisions.
Virginia	Not specifically delegated; presumably vested in Alcoholic Beverage Control Board.	Agents of the Alcoholic Beverage Control Board and local law enforcement officers.	Attorneys of the Commonwealth.	Alcoholic Beverage Control Board.	No appeal may be taken.
Washington	Liquor Control Board and the Attorney General of the state as General Counsel of the Board.	Enforcement officers of the Liquor Control Board and county and municipal police officers.	Attorney General of the state.	Liquor Control Board.	No appeal may be taken.
West Virginia	Liquor: members of Liquor Control Commission and officers, agents, and employees of the Commission. Beer: Non-intoxicating Beer Commissioner.	Liquor: agents of the Liquor Control Commission and all peace officers. Beer: agents of Non-intoxicating Beer Commissioner.	Liquor: Attorney General or the state and county prosecuting attorneys. Beer: Attorney General or the state and county prosecuting attorneys.	Liquor: Liquor Control Commission. Beer: Non-intoxicating Beer Commissioner.	Liquor: Liquor license appeals to appropriate court of jurisdiction. Beer: Non-intoxicating beer license appeals to Circuit Court of Kanawha County.
Wisconsin	Not specifically delegated; presumably vested in local issuing authorities and State Treasurer.	Local police officers, sheriffs, and constables; in some cases employees of State Treasurer.	District attorneys.	Local issuing body or court of record in county in which premises located; state may also bring revocation proceedings.	Court of record in county in which premises are located for appeals from actions of local issuing authorities.
Wyoming	Not specifically delegated; presumably vested in State Liquor Commission and local issuing authorities.	Agents of the State Liquor Commission and other state law enforcement officers, and city, town, and county law enforcement officers.	Every prosecuting attorney in the state.	State Liquor Commission and respective local licensing authorities.	District court of county in which premises are located.
District of Columbia	Not specifically delegated; presumably vested in Alcoholic Beverage Control Board.	Members of the ABC Board or its agents and metropolitan police.	Corporation Counsel of District of Columbia or his assistants, or U. S. Attorney or his assistants.	Alcoholic Beverage Control Board.	Commissioners of the District of Columbia.

[a] Revocation by Liquor Control Commission is mandatory upon request of local governmental units.
[b] Appellate procedures not applicable to decision of State Board of Alcoholic Control.

123

TABLE 19

METHODS USED BY STATE ABC AGENCIES TO INSTRUCT LOCAL LAW OFFICERS AND EVALUATE LOCAL ENFORCEMENT

(As Reported in Questionnaire Replies)

State	Methods Used by State ABC Agencies to Instruct Local Law Officers in ABC Law Enforcement				Methods Used by State ABC Agencies to Evaluate Local Enforcement		States in Which Local Jurisdictions Submit Regular Reports to the State ABC Agency Concerning Violations Related to the Operation of Licensed Premises
	Issuance of Instructional Pamphlet or Guidebook	Conduct of Training Courses	Systematic Visits by a State Agent	Special Informational Releases to Local Police Units	Investigation of Complaints from the Public	Systematic Inspection of all Licensed Premises	
Alabama	X	—	X	—	X	X	—
Arkansas	—	—	—	—	X	—	—
California	X	a	—	—	—	—	—
Colorado	X	—	X	X	X	X	X
Connecticut	X	—	X	X	X	X	X
Delaware	—	—	—	—	X	X	X
Florida	X	—	X	—	X	X	—
Georgia	—	—	X	—	X	X	—
Idaho	—	X	—	X	X	X	—
Illinois	—	—	—	—	X	X	—
Indiana	—	X	X	X	X	X	X
Iowa	—	—	—	—	X	—	X
Kentucky	—	—	X	—	X	X	X
Maryland	—	—	—	—	X	X	X
Michigan	X	X	X	X	X	X	X
Minnesota	—	—	X	X	X	X	—
Missouri	—	—	—	X	X	X	—
Nebraska	—	—	X	—	—	X	—
Nevada	—	—	—	—	—	—	—
New Hampshire	—	—	—	—	—	—	—
New Jersey	—	—	—	X	X	X	X
New Mexico	—	—	—	—	X	X	—
New York	X	X	X	X	Xb	Xc	X
North Carolina	—	X	—	—	—	X	X
North Dakota	—	—	X	—	X	X	—
Ohio	—	—	—	X	X	X	—
Oregon	—	—	X	—	X	X	—
Pennsylvania	—	—	X	X	—	—	—
Rhode Island	X	—	—	—	X	X	X
South Carolina	—	—	—	—	—	—	X
South Dakota	—	—	—	—	—	—	—
Vermont	—	X	X	X	X	X	X
Virginia	—	—	X	X	X	X	X
Washington	—	—	X	—	X	X	—
West Virginia	—	—	X	—	X	X	—
Wisconsin	—	—	—	—	—	—	X
District of Columbia	—	X	—	—	X	X	—

a Training courses are available for local law enforcement personnel but are not required.
b Spot checking only; most complaints referred to local police.
c Through Local ABC Boards.

TABLE 20

POWERS OF ARREST, AND OF ENTRY WITHOUT WARRANT, OF STATE ABC ENFORCEMENT AGENTS

(As Reported by Questionnaire Replies)

State	Do Agents Have Power of Arrest?	Do Agents Have Right of Entry of Licensed Premises without Warrant?
Alabama	Yes	No
Arkansas	No	No
California	Yes	Yes
Colorado	Yes	Yes
Connecticut	No	Yes
Delaware	Yes	Yes
Florida	Yes	Yes
Georgia	Yes	Yes
Idaho	Yes	Yes
Illinois	No	No
Indiana	Yes	Yes
Iowa	a	a b
Kentucky	Yes	Yes
Maryland	No	Yes
Michigan	No	Yes
Minnesota	No	No
Missouri	Yes	Yes
Nebraska	Yes	Yes
Nevada	No	No
New Hampshire	Yes	No
New Jersey	Yes	Yes
New Mexico	Yes	No
New York	No	Yes
North Carolina	Yes	No
North Dakota	Yes	Yes
Ohio	Yes	Yes
Oregon	Yes	Yes
Pennsylvania	Yes	Yes
Rhode Island	No	Yes
South Carolina	Yes	Yes
South Dakota	No	No
Vermont	Yes	No
Virginia	Yes	Yes
Washington	Yes	Yes
West Virginia—Liquor	Yes	No
Beer	No	Yes
Wisconsin	Yes	Yes
District of Columbia	No	Yes

a The Iowa Liquor Control Commission does not have the duty of enforcing the Liquor laws of the state (State v. Cooper, 265 NW 915), and cannot assign any of its personnel to assist local law enforcement officers (A. G. Opin., May 29, 1936).

b Presumably, enforcement personnel have the right to enter and inspect licensed premises at any time such premises are open for business. The replies tabulated here are interpreted to mean the right of entry, search and seizure at any time without warrant.

TABLE 21

STATES IN WHICH ABC LAWS AND/OR RULES ASSIGN RECORD-KEEPING FUNCTIONS TO LICENSEES, BY CLASSES OF LICENSEES

State	Manufacturers	Transporters	Wholesalers, Distributors, Etc.	Retailers
Alabama	X	X	X	X
Arizona	X	—	X	X
Arkansas	X	X	X	X
California	X	a	X	X
Colorado	X	—	X	X
Connecticut	X	X	X	X
Delaware	a	—	—	X
Florida	X	X	X	—
Georgia	X	a	X	X
Idaho	X	a	X	X
Illinois	X	a	X	X
Indiana	X	—	X	—
Iowa	X	—	X	X
Kansas	X	—	X	X
Kentucky	X	X	X	X
Louisiana	X	X	X	X
Maine	X	—	X	X
Maryland	X	X	X	X
Massachusetts	X	—	X	—
Michigan	X	—	X	—
Minnesota	X	X	X	X
Missouri	X	—	X	X
Montana	X	—	X	X
Nebraska	X	a	X	a
Nevada	—	X	X	X
New Hampshire	a	—	a	—
New Jersey	X	X	X	X
New Mexico	—	—	—	X
New York	X	X	X	X
North Carolina	X	X	X	X
North Dakota	a	—	X	—
Ohio	X	—	X	X
Oregon	X	X	X	—
Pennsylvania	X	X	X	X
Rhode Island	—	—	X	X
South Carolina	X	—	X	X
South Dakota	X	—	X	—
Tennessee	X	—	X	X
Texas	X	a	X	X
Utah	X	—	X	—
Vermont	a	—	a	—
Virginia	X	—	X	X
Washington	X	—	X	X
West Virginia	X	—	X	—
Wisconsin	X	—	X	X
Wyoming	a	—	a	—
District of Columbia	X	—	X	X

a Keeping of records not specifically required, but licensees must submit detailed report as to inventories and /or transactions.

TABLE 22

SIZE OF STATE ABC ENFORCEMENT STAFFS AND VOLUME OF STATE ABC ENFORCEMENT ACTIONS

(As Reported in Questionnaire Replies Covering Last Fiscal Year)

State	No. of State ABC Enforcement Personnel	Do State Police or Traffic Patrols Participate in ABC Enforcement?	No. of Retail Licenses Revoked by State ABC Agencies During Last Fiscal Year	No. of Retail Licenses Suspended by State ABC Agencies During Last Fiscal Year	No. of Arrests for Violations of State ABC Laws Made by State Law Enforcement Authorities During Last Fiscal Year	No. of ABC Law Violation Cases Referred by State ABC Agencies to Prosecuting Officers for Court Trial During Last Fiscal Year
Alabama	67	No	15	10	4028	—
Arkansas	3	b	32	0	—	—
California	275	No	57	618	434	434
Colorado	10	No	3	59	8	8
Connecticut	18	Yes	14	88	—	—
Delaware	10	Yes	0	10	15	—
Florida	84	No	30	40	1843	—
Georgia	75	Yes	0	0	2485	2485
Idaho	10	No	0	0	—	—
Illinois	42	No	0 d	59	0	99
Indiana	83	Yes	29	297	1445	1304
Iowa	0	Yes	0 d	0	2200 h	—
Kentucky	27	c	10	30	—	—
Maryland	13	b	d	306	3	4
Michigan	90	Yes	26	410	—	—
Minnesota	15	No	0	0	0	342
Missouri	50	c	46	326	273	273
Nebraska	17	No	6	49	—	—
Nevada	0	Yes	—	0	0	0
New Hampshire	17	No	1	51	31	31
New Jersey	100	Yes	14	155 f	170	170
New Mexico	7	Yes	4	4	—	0
New York	20 (approximately)	Yes	258 e	221	0 i	275
North Carolina	16	Yes	0	0	—	—
North Dakota	6	No	6	72	10	10
Ohio	110	No	183	283	937	937
Oregon	63	No	28	111	361	361
Pennsylvania	340	c	79	759	709	702
Rhode Island	11	Yes	1	19 g	—	—
South Carolina	9	Yes	98	99	1178	0
South Dakota	a	No	—	0	—	—
Vermont	9	Yes	1	27	17	44
Virginia	107	Yes	101	104	2354	2026
Washington	72	No	15	116	443	0
West Virginia	32	Yes	37	139	332	48
Wisconsin	30	No	1	0	276	276
District of Columbia	10	Yes	4	33	—	0

a Field men of Division of Taxation administering various kinds of state taxes perform all state enforcement work with respect to alcoholic beverages.

b Law provides for participation by state police; questionnaire indicates that state police do not generally participate in ABC enforcement activities.

c Only upon request as for special raids, etc.

d Local licensing authorities are primarily responsible for retail license revocations.

e Includes involuntary termination by cancellation or revocation.

f Local law enforcement authorities suspended 186 licenses during same period.

g Local law enforcement authorities suspended 19 licenses during same period.

h Probably refers to arrests made by local law enforcement authorities.

i Local law enforcement authorities made 242 arrests during same period.